The Course of This World

The Course of This World

LESLEE KISER

I'd like to thank Brandon for his love and support. Besides being devastatingly handsome, he loves God more than me, and there's nothing I need more in our marriage than that.

I'd like to dedicate this book to dear friends of mine, Jackie and Lisa Ezell, for teaching my husband and I and introducing us to The Hill Ministries and B.A.S.I.C. Training. God used you to change our lives, and we'll be forever grateful.

I'd like to give a special thanks to Dana Morrow, Jolene Sloan, Julie Penual, Lavedia Edwards, Lorie Patterson, and TeriAnn Hooper. I prayed for months leading up to our focus group that God would handpick His team to speak truth into my life and this book. He came through in a big way with y'all. Your time, input, and friendship means more to me than I can ever put into words.
Love y'all!

Table of Contents

Introduction

Let me start by saying I'm so excited for you to seek God. I hope this book will give you a deeper desire to know Him more intimately. I don't want you to think the following pages are about me, so I'm going to try not to talk much about myself. But if I do, it's to give you some insight into how I got here.

My husband, Brandon, was on the way home from a football game and heard some preacher on the radio. He called me and said, "You gotta hear this guy!" We found his church online and started listening to some sermons. Shortly after that, we decided to be at our church when the doors opened, or at least we'd attend more consistently because before hearing the passion in this man's preaching, we were only going when we felt like it…and you know how that goes.

We didn't realize it at the time, but God was working in our hearts. The Holy Spirit was preparing us to want more of Him. Our lives changed forever because of it, even though we didn't realize it until much later.

A few months after attending more regularly, we met Jackie and Lisa. They were a new couple that had just moved in down the street. After being around them a little more, we began to notice there was just something different about them. When we found out Jackie was a Bible teacher, we decided to attend one of his classes and *bam*! We never knew scripture could be so engaging. God used Jackie to show us how to seek His heart.

I grew up in the church we were attending. That church will always hold a special place in my heart because it was an avenue for salvation. However, looking back, I realize that nobody actually walked me through what to do after trusting Jesus as my Lord and Savior. I was taught a lot about the stories in the Bible but very little about the God who wrote it. The Lord used Jackie to draw us to God, see His heart, and teach us how to study the love letter He wrote to us. His passion to know God's heart was contagious, and we couldn't get enough.

The Course of This World is about four years in the making. One goal for this book is to glorify the Father. It's written for what He gets out of it. I'm called to be obedient and share what He's shown me, but the results are up to *Him*. If you see my passion for the

Father and let the Holy Spirit light a fire in you to know God on a personal level, *great*. If not, that's okay too. Another goal is to expose the enemy and his lies so we can learn to defeat him.

My hope is that you'll take the information you learn and let it create real change. I've worked through studies where I've completed the homework, discussed it in class, then put it on the shelf and never thought about it again. Forgetting about the material is easy to do. What's *not* easy is to be 100 percent honest with yourself, take time to ponder what God is trying to show you, and give Him the opportunity to use it to mature you spiritually.

I'll also throw some juicy little tidbits (JLTs) in here in hopes you'll want to dig deeper into who God is. I get sidetracked sometimes when I'm reading and end up chasing rabbits, but it's in those moments that He reveals the truth to me. I love it when that happens and pray you'll give the Lord time alone, in His word, to show you too.

Author's note: all quoted scripture verses are from the 1977 edition of the New American Standard Bible (NASB) unless otherwise stated.

WEEK 1
Day 1
Life as We Know It

We're born, we learn to walk and talk, and we spend the rest of our lives looking forward to the next opportunity. When we're in grade school, we can't wait to get to middle school. When we're in high school, we can't wait to get a job and start making money. When we're established in our careers, we can't wait to retire. From birth to death, we spend our years looking for something else, something bigger and better no matter how much we accomplish. Have you experienced this never-ending cycle of searching? Have you ever looked at your life and thought, "There's got to be more than this!"? Me too.

I've heard people talk about "God's plan" for our lives and how He has one for everybody. What I've learned in the past few years is that Satan also has a plan for us. It's simple. The devil's one and only goal is to keep us from God. But before we can talk about his strategy, we've got to know who we're up against.

Look up Ephesians 2:1–2 and write it out below.

Now underline "the course of this world."

Satan's plan for humanity *is* the "course of this world" the verses talk about. They go on to say that we *"formerly lived in the lusts of our flesh, indulging the desires of the flesh and of the mind"* (Eph. 2:3). So, his design for us is to live in the lusts of our flesh and mind and to continue to be children of wrath.

But first, how did we become children of wrath, and who *is* Satan?

Let's go back to the beginning to find the answer. Look up Genesis 2:16–17 and note anything that stands out to you.

God told Adam he could eat of any tree in the garden, *"but from the tree of the knowledge of good and evil you shall not eat, for in the day that you eat from it you shall surely die"* (Gen. 2:17). You probably know the rest of the story, but if not, Eve ate the forbidden fruit, gave it to Adam, and he ate it too. But guess what? They didn't die! At least, they didn't die physically. Adam and Eve experienced a spiritual death (Gen. 3:7).

> **JLT #1**—In Genesis 2:17, when God told Adam what he could and couldn't eat, Eve wasn't on the scene yet. The Lord didn't create her until Genesis 2:22. Have you ever wondered why the serpent went to her first? Maybe it was because she wasn't there for the actual instructions and only heard them secondhand from Adam. Adam got the real lowdown; Eve simply heard his version, and you know that when news spreads, it rarely ends up like it started, even if there are only two of you.

God gave clear guidelines on what they could and couldn't do. You can eat whatever you want…except from this one tree. If you have kids, you know telling them what *not* to do only makes them want to do it more, right? The serpent shows up and approaches Eve. He places doubt in her mind by saying (and I'm paraphrasing here), "That might be what God *said*, but this is what He *really* meant. He's holding out on you. You won't die. You'll become like Him." Satan has a way of lying, doesn't he? He spins the truth just enough to get us to question or doubt God.

Do you ever doubt God?

Do you think it's okay to doubt or question the Creator?

After Adam and Eve sinned, or "after the Fall" as some Bible scholars refer to it, God banished Adam and Eve from the Garden of Eden. He put a cherub around the tree of life to guard it so they couldn't eat it anymore. Before the Fall, God didn't care if they consumed its fruit because they were sinless. After, since they were dead spiritually, eating from it would've made them stay in that spiritually dead state for all eternity (Gen. 3:22). But God wouldn't leave them like that. He had a plan.

Genesis 3:14–19 spells it out. Read those verses and see if you can write His plan below.

The Lord's plan is as follows: The serpent (Satan) is cursed (verse 14). There will be enmity between the woman's seed (first reference to Jesus) and Satan's (verse 15a). He'll bruise you on the head, and you'll bruise Him on the heel (first reference of the suffering Savior; verse 15b). Essentially, God would send Christ to save the world from its fallen state.

Romans 5:12 discusses the world's fallen condition. *"Therefore, just as through one man sin entered into the world, and death through sin, and so death spread to all men, because all sinned."*

God created man in His image, but since Adam chose to defy God's perfect design, all humans from then on were and are born with an Adamic nature, or spiritually dead. That's what Ephesians 2:1 is talking about when it refers to us being dead in our trespasses and sins. It means we're born without a desire to please God. The concept of pleasing God is foreign to humans who are not yet born again. Have you ever wondered how nonbelievers can continuously sin and think nothing of it? They do so because sinning to them is as natural as breathing. It was to us, too, before we met Jesus.

Think about it. When a baby is born, it's helpless. Young children learn early on that when they cry, somebody comes to their aid. They're hungry, they cry, and they get fed. They have a dirty diaper, they cry, and they get it changed. We're born with a natural instinct to get *our* needs met. That doesn't sound so bad, right?

Imagine acting like a baby at work, in church, or at home with your family. You're an adult, but every time you want or need something, you cry until somebody gets it for you. Doesn't that sound ridiculous?

When we trust Jesus as Lord and Savior, we become babies in Christ. We've just been born of a new nature, but one that only wants to please God. It's weird, different from what we're used to, and takes some time to figure out. Unfortunately, in some churches today, new believers aren't being told what to do after they're saved. Preachers and teachers will congratulate you and send you on your merry way. Can you imagine how the world would be if we did the same to actual babies? Welcome to the world; now go figure it out. They wouldn't survive long, would they? Well, "baby" Christians have a hard time too. We possess a new nature but act the same.

Did you think that once you got saved everything would magically change? That you would no longer want to do the same things you used to?

What are some things you still have a hard time *not* doing?

The problem is we've been on "this course" of choosing sin for so long that we've formed general ways of living called habits, or what I like to call our default settings. These habit patterns feel natural to us because they define us, right? *Wrong.* Once you're in Christ as a new believer, what you do is not who you are, though who you are has a great deal of influence on what you do.

This course the enemy has us on from birth has developed in us these default settings like a computer. When a computer is first manufactured, it has programs that automatically run because it was designed to operate that way. The longer we stay on the course of this world, the more default settings we create. We'll talk more about that later, but let's continue to discover who Satan is.

Once upon a time, there was a being who was great in God's eyes. Read Ezekiel 28:12–15a and Isaiah 14:12, and record what you notice about this individual below.

Ezekiel 28:12b–15a tells us that Lucifer was God's anointed cherub who guarded the throne of God (28:14). He was perfect, wise, and beautiful. God called him *"blameless in your ways from the day you were created"* (28:15a). So, what happened?

Ezekiel 28:15b–16 provides the explanation: *"Until unrighteousness was found in you. By the abundance of your trade you were internally filled with violence, and you sinned."*

Isaiah 14:13–14 describes Satan's downfall this way, *"But you said in your heart, 'I will ascend to heaven; I will raise my throne above the stars of God, and I will sit on the mount of the assembly in the recesses of the north. I will ascend above the heights of the clouds; I will make myself like the Most High.'"*

Notice anything about the Isaiah passages?

There are many "I" statements in those verses. Satan began to think he was really something. God made him beautiful, successful, and prosperous. He thought to himself, and I'm paraphrasing again: "Man, everybody respects me. I'm next in line under God, so I'll go ahead and promote myself above the stars and put myself in His position. After all, I've got the seal of perfection from God Himself" (Ezek. 28:11–15a).

Satan's pride got the best of him. It wasn't fair for everybody to worship God when he was just as perfect and blameless. What a scary place to be…thinking you're better than the Father. Y'all, pride kills.

God, may You rid us of our pride before it takes hold of our lives like it did Satan's. In Jesus's name, amen!

Keep reading through Ezekiel 28:17–19.

To summarize, Satan continued exalting himself, and because of it, his wisdom became corrupted. Think about that for a minute. Does that mean that when we think too highly of ourselves, our wisdom diminishes? *Yes.* Do these thoughts sound familiar: "I need to revamp my wardrobe," "I'm over this haircut; I need a new, more fabulous one," or "I need a new purse because everybody's got this one now." You end up thinking way *more* about yourself and way *less* about God.

Can you think of anything that causes you to think more about you and less about Him? Let's make a list:

The problem is that when we spend more time thinking about ourselves, we'll suffer the consequences for it. The enemy loves unaligned priorities because the more distracted he can make you, the less time God has to effect change in your life.

So, what happened next? God took Satan from the holy mountain and threw him down to the ground so that all who saw him would be appalled (Ezek. 28:17–19). Isaiah 14:12b states, *"You have been cut down to the earth."*

When God created the heavens and the earth, He crafted them to operate in perfect harmony, including man. Adam and Eve were naked and unashamed (Gen. 2:25). The earth was perfect, man's role on earth was flawless, and everything was great. In Genesis 2:15, God took Adam and put him in the garden to cultivate and keep it.

JLT #2—The Hebrew word for "cultivate" is *abad* and means "work," but there is no connotation with toilsome labor.[1] "Abad" implies a joyful experience of liberation. The word for "keep" is *shamar* and means "to watch over, guard, or protect."[2] God's original design for man was to enjoy his work. Adam would have been ecstatic to please God by keeping His garden looking fresh.

However, since sin entered humans, everything changed. Work became burdensome, difficult, and filled with opposition (Gen. 3:17–19). Childbirth would be much more painful (3:16), and there would also be a disconnect in the relationship between husband and wife. Verse 16 starts by saying childbirth will be more painful, then says, *"Yet your desire shall be for your husband"* and finishes with, *"and he shall rule over you."* The word for desire here means "unhealthy longing." The sequence of the verse leads me to think that having children will no longer be enough to fulfill a woman's life. She'll have an "unhealthy longing" for her husband, or in context, his authority over her. The point of the story is that sin tarnished God's perfect design.

Do you love your job (even if it's being a stay-at-home mom)?

Do you have a heavenly perspective about it? Why or why not?

---

[1] Strong's Concordance, s.v. "abad," accessed April 18, 2022, https://biblehub.com/hebrew/5647.htm.

[2] Strong's Concordance, s.v. "shamar," accessed April 18, 2022, https://biblehub.com/hebrew/8104.htm.

Ever since God cast Satan down to earth and revealed His plan of salvation (Gen. 3:14–19), the devil has been coming up with ways to mess it all up. Here are some ways the Bible describes him:

- The serpent—craftier than any other beast of the field (Gen. 3:1).
- The adversary—brings accusations about us to God (Job 1:6–12).
- The accuser—(Rev. 12:10).
- The god of the age—who blinds the minds of unbelievers so they can't see (2 Cor. 4:4).
- The prince of the power of the air—who works in the sons of disobedience (Eph. 2:2).

When Satan tempted Jesus after He was baptized, he took Him and showed Him all the kingdoms of the world and said, "*I will give You all this domain and its glory*" (Luke 4:6). It alludes to Satan's power over the earth, even if it's only for a short time (Rev. 12:12).

He knows that if we spend time with God and let Him change our hearts, we'll draw others to Him for the good of the kingdom. Satan's daily ritual is to do whatever it takes to keep us away from the Lord. He *hates* when we give the Holy Spirit time to teach us. He *hates* when we pray. He *hates* when we talk to others about God. You see the point. The devil wants to keep us from all things related to the Father however he can.

That's where our disposition for sin comes into play. We briefly discussed Romans 5:12 before, where it says that all have sinned. Let's see what catering to sinful nature (before we were saved) looks like in real life.

Read 1 Kings 21:1–4. How did Ahab cater to his flesh?

King Ahab wanted a vineyard that belonged to somebody else. He offered Naboth, the owner, another vineyard and money. Naboth told him, "*The LORD forbid me that I should give you the inheritance of my fathers*" (1 Kings 21:3). Ahab went home and pouted like a spoiled brat. He threw a hissy fit and went to bed without eating because he didn't get his way. His wife, Jezebel, couldn't believe he was sulking. After all, he was the king! She told him she'd take care of it for him (21:7) and developed a plan. She executed her plan, which was to have Naboth killed and give Ahab possession of the vineyard.

There are consequences for sin in your life on earth, and they never just affect you.

Who else did Ahab's selfishness impact?

Do you have sins in your life that you see affecting others?

God, as we go through life on earth, may You go before us and open our hearts, minds, eyes, and ears to Your word. May You take this information and make it revelation, writing it on our hearts as we seek You. In Jesus's name, amen!

Day 2
Sets of Threes

As we dive into today's study, we're going to learn about three stages of believers. In the New Testament, 1 John 2 talks about the categories. Verse 12 says, *"I am writing to you, **little children**, because your sins are forgiven you for His name's sake."* Verses 13b and 14b say, *"I am writing you, **young men**, because you have overcome the evil one."* And finally, verses 13a and 14a say, *"I am writing to you, **fathers**, because you know Him who has been from the beginning."*

- **Little children** have been saved. They're out of hell and into heaven, but that's all they've learned so far. When adversity comes, because they've not quite figured out how to endure it, they look and act just like the rest of the world. They usually start out so excited because the Lord has saved them, but since they've not yet understood what to do next, they get frustrated and can eventually burn out. These are spiritual babies who are in it for what they get out of it.
- **Young men** are learning how to deal with adversity. The verse says they've overcome the evil one. Once we cry out to God and ask Him to forgive us our sins and come into our hearts and be our Savior, He frees us from the power of our sin. The power of sin is what the enemy uses to put sinful thoughts in our heads, the ones that condemn our person and convince us that we're dirty, rotten, no-good sinners whom God could never love. They are the very thoughts that keep us focused on anything and everything other than Him. Young men have learned to recognize and reject these sinful thoughts.
- **Fathers** know the Lord—Creator of all who has been here from the beginning. Fathers are a rare find. These are people who, as a byproduct of knowing God intimately, have learned to continuously live by the life of another, just like Jesus did while He was on earth. According to John 14:10, Jesus did nothing of His own initiative but lived by the Father's life abiding in Him. We'll never be sinless on this side of heaven, but the more time we spend with God, the closer we can get. These fathers, *"who because of practice,*

have their senses trained to discern good and evil" (Heb. 5:14), can see things from His perspective and respond accordingly. Because they continually dig out truth for themselves and beg God to teach them straight from His heart to theirs, they're able to make decisions based on what He gets out of it.

As we journey through this study together, we'll hopefully start to learn how to move through the steps John discusses. We'll uncover what the enemy does to distract us and how to prevent it. My goal is for you to expose the schemes of the devil and learn how to defeat him.

What leads you away from the Lord? Think about it and see if you can already spot some things that get in the way. We'll come back to this topic later.

There are three categories of sin and three things that tempt us to sin. All sin falls into one of these types (1 John 2:16):

- Lust of the flesh
- Lust of the eyes
- The boastful pride of life

The three things that tempt us are:

- The world
- The flesh
- The devil

God, as we take our first look into the categories all sins fit into, I ask You to lead our conversations, questions, and private study times to where You are. May You take us down rabbit holes that lead to Your truth so it can transform our lives. In Jesus's name, amen.

Day 3
The Lust of the Flesh

Take a few minutes to read Luke 4:1–4.

Jesus was in the wilderness for forty days, and during that time, He ate nothing. After the evil one tempted Him, He became hungry. Satan said, and I'm paraphrasing again, "Hey, Man, it's been forty days since You ate last. You must be starved! Just make these stones into bread and dig in." Satan was appealing to Christ's flesh.

What desire of the flesh is the hardest for you to resist?

The lust of the flesh can be many things. For me, I get the urge at least once a day to eat a pint of Phish Food. If you don't know what that is, good. If you do, you're probably in the same boat as me...forever fighting my flesh to eat healthy foods instead of what I want. Desires of the flesh could be an obsession to be physically fit, to fulfill sexual fantasies, or to drown your sorrows in a bottle. Generally, it's satisfying your desire and is just for you.

Most of the time, we fall for the thought that if it "feels right," it must be okay. The enemy has convinced us that pleasing ourselves before or instead of looking out for others is acceptable. However, giving in to those thoughts or feelings can come with consequences. Sometimes those outcomes might be seemingly harmless, like gaining five pounds. Other times, they can be drastic, like having an unplanned child at a young age or being a convicted felon.

Romans 8:6–7 states, *"The mind set on the flesh is death, but the mind set on the Spirit is life and peace, because the mind set on the flesh is hostile toward God; for it does not subject itself to the law of God, for it is not even able to do so."*

Let's keep that in mind as we read the NASB translation of 2 Samuel 13. I know this is a long chapter, but it's worth it.

What do you see in the passage about pleasing the flesh?

I bring this story to your attention because it underscores the dangers of succumbing to the flesh. Amnon was "in love" with his sister, so much so that he made himself sick over it. His buddy, Jonadab, asked him, and I'm still paraphrasing, "What's the deal? Why are you so depressed all the time?" (2 Sam. 13:4). When he heard what was going on, he came up with a plan to get his friend the girl of his dreams.

His strategy worked like a charm until Amnon said to Tamar, "*Come, lie with me, my sister.*" (2 Sam. 13:11). She freaked out, begged him not to violate her, and told him all he had to do was ask the king for her hand in marriage and he'd give her to him (13:12–13). Amnon refused, and since he was stronger than her, he slept with her against her will (13:14).

The end is the part I want you to see, 2 Samuel 13:15, which states, "*Then Amnon hated her with a very great hatred; for the hatred with which he hated her was greater than the love with which he had loved her. And Amnon said to her, 'Get up, go away!'*"

The very thing you *think* you love will be the thing you hate after you get it. And not only that, but you will also hate it more than you thought you loved it. This is a crucial lesson for us all to learn, young and old. Feelings and emotions can cloud your judgment. The enemy knows that and uses it against you.

I've noticed when I've had a bad day, I think to myself, "I'm going to go home, get a Swiss cake roll, and binge-watch my shows. I can't possibly make any more decisions; I just need to turn off my brain for a while." The very thing my flesh is telling me to do (turn off my brain) is the one thing that can protect me from the enemy's attacks. Turning my brain off will keep me in the dark, separated from godly thinking.

What do you turn to when you've had a bad day?

Does the way you comfort yourself keep you in the dark? Or draw you near to God?

If I seek Him instead and spend time in the scriptures, He can begin to show me how to combat bad days with truth. Plus, eating a bunch of junk will allow me to run to food for my comfort instead of the Lord, who is the only source of fulfillment that can and does last. Our flesh urges us to do things that will keep us in a never-ending spiral because if we stay there, we won't mature spiritually or impact others for God.

Can you pinpoint some triggers that keep you in the dark?

So, what do we do about it? From 2 Corinthians 10:5, we read, "We are *destroying speculations and every lofty thing raised up against the knowledge of God, and* we are *taking every thought captive to the obedience of Christ.*" Did you know that just because a thought comes into your head doesn't mean you have to believe or act on it?

Oh God, I cry out to You today for these women who have taken time to seek You through this book. May You make it real to them, teach them to question suspicious thoughts that come into their minds, and give them the ability to tell themselves no when their flesh wants too much. In Jesus's name, amen.

Day 4
The Lust of the Eyes (Comparison Kills)

This idea seems simple: you have a strong desire for what you see. It could be as easy as Naboth's vineyard from 1 Kings. It could be your coworker's position in the company. It could be the obvious choice of lusting after somebody you think is attractive. Can you think of anywhere in the Bible where lust of the eyes got somebody in trouble?

Read 2 Samuel 11 and note what lust of the flesh occurs.

The story is about the great King David, the man after God's own heart (1 Sam. 13:14). I believe at that point in his life, he was a "young man," spiritually speaking. He saw things from a heavenly perspective early on (1 Sam. 17:26, 45–46) and was able to defeat the enemy most of the time. That's the thing with the enemy, though; he's relentless. If you're seeking God, he'll constantly try to distract you. He'll attempt everything until he finds a weakness. David's weakness was a beautiful woman.

David was supposed to be in battle but stayed home (2 Sam. 11:1). He was on the rooftop of his palace and noticed Bathsheba bathing. He should've taken his sinful thoughts captive, gone inside, and stopped looking at her. Instead, he inquired about her, met her, and had sex with her (11:3–4). She became pregnant, and he freaked out! Her husband, Uriah, was in his army and was so loyal that when David called him home to be with her, he slept at the door of the king's house instead.

When David asked him why he did that, he said, *"The ark and Israel and Judah are staying in temporary shelters, and my lord Joab and the servants of my lord are camping in the open field. Shall I then go to my house to eat and drink and to lie with my wife? By your life and the life of your soul, I will not do this thing"* (11:11).

David's plan was to bring Uriah home and let him sleep with his wife so that when he found out she was pregnant, he would think the child was his. Sounds like an episode of *Jerry Springer*, right? But Uriah was too loyal for that, so David had to be creative. He gave orders to Joab, the commander of his army, to put him on the front lines and make sure he didn't come home. Enemy soldiers killed Uriah in battle, and David took Bathsheba as his wife.

In this world of convenience, video games that desensitize us to killing and death, and the overwhelming amount of technology and social media, it's easy to make decisions just like David made. Society has hypnotized us to believe "we deserve it" and "YOLO." In these selfish attitudes, we'll do anything to get what *we* want.

Can you think of a decision you've made to get something you just had to have, something you couldn't live without?

When you got it, did it make you happy?

If so, did that happiness last?

Like I said before, there are going to be consequences in life on earth, and for David, they were devastating. First, Nathan the prophet told him the sword would never depart from his house (2 Sam. 12:10). Second, he'd lose his wives, and they'd be given to his companions to lie with them in broad daylight (12:11). Finally, the child conceived during his sinful act would die (12:14). David's sin affected his other wives, his friends who took them in broad daylight, Bathsheba, and most of all, the child born because of their sin.

Y'all, his story is extreme and devastating, but let it be a testament to God's grace. God didn't leave David in his mess. That's the thing about being a forgiven child of God. He'll call out your sin and let you decide how to deal with it; we do have a choice. We can wallow in self-pity like Ahab, or we can repent and ask God to help us recover from those failures and give us insight so we never go there again. If we choose to repent and follow God's route, we mature spiritually. The more we do that, the easier choosing His way will become, and we'll hopefully begin to recognize the enemy's ridiculous thoughts in time to say *no*.

JLT #3—As we see in David's story, sin never just affects you. Read Joshua 7. It's a story about Achan. God gave specific instructions not to keep anything from the city of Jericho. The town was under the ban, and the spoils belonged to the Lord (Josh. 6:17–18). But Achan saw some things in Jericho that he wanted, so he took them (Josh. 7:20–

21). Achan, his sons, daughters, oxen, donkeys, sheep, tent, and all that belonged to him were stoned and burned. His sin affected everything and everybody he loved.

Read 2 Samuel 12:1–23. That passage is the whole story of when David's sin found him out. Nathan called David out for his transgressions (2 Sam. 12:7). David's choice on how to respond was to go to God. He prayed in desperation, knowing that he'd broken God's heart.

Read Psalm 51 and record below what you see. How did he talk to God about what he'd done?

We have a choice on how to respond to our sin. Being honest with yourself here can lead to growth even though it'll probably hurt to admit your failures. Remember, nobody else will see this. It's just you and God.

What's your typical response to sin in your life? Is it brokenness or blame? Is it repentance or bitterness? Do you talk to God about how to move forward, or do you wallow in it way too long?

As we mature spiritually, we should look to God and heavenly things. When we take our eyes off God and start looking around us, we see that we're different than others. The Lord planned for every single person to be unique, but as we're learning, the enemy tells us something different. Once he fills our heads with lies, we tend to hate our differences and wish to change or hide them. Seeing that we're different than everybody else can lead to comparison, which can lead us to…

- Consider options we didn't know we had
- Consider too many options
- Make assumptions
- Become a follower
- Question everything

The first result of comparison is considering options you didn't know you had. Read Genesis 3:1–7 and see what happens when we take that route.

We've talked about Adam and Eve already, but now let's focus on the fact that they were perfectly happy until the serpent showed them another angle. God told them to eat whatever they wanted except from that one tree because if they did, they'd die. They were fine with avoiding the tree of knowledge of good and evil. Well, they were until the enemy placed doubt in Eve's mind. He convinced her that God was hiding something from her, that she wouldn't die if she ate the fruit, but she'd become like Him. Before that conversation, they accepted God's word as an absolute and abided by it. Then the enemy exposed them to other options.

That's what he does. He puts ideas into our heads that will sidetrack us. What the enemy said was true. They didn't die physically. God never said the tree *wasn't* good for food, delightful to look at, or that it'd make them wise. He simply said not to eat from it. Satan exposed Adam and Eve to options God hadn't meant for them to see.

Have you noticed yourself considering options you shouldn't?

Here are some that might come to mind:

- Living with a significant other before marriage
- Eating past the point of nutrition simply because what you're eating tastes good
- Suicide

These examples may seem scattered, but I want you to think about something. I grew up in the Bible Belt, in the Southeast, where there was a church on just about every corner. In my sheltered little world when I was growing up, my parents kept things from me to try and protect me. They didn't tell me that people could live together and have sex before marriage because they wanted me to assume the only way to get all that was to be married.

When I was young, I would see a huge pile of candy, and all I'd want to do was eat it until there was no more. When we're a little older and have more experience under our belts, we understand that more options come with more consequences. If we eat all the candy, we're most likely going to have a stomachache and may even get sick. Sometimes, our elders hide other options from us because we're not mature enough to rationally consider them.

The enemy also leaves out what the consequences will be if we choose sin. He *always* does that because if we knew that taking that first bite of cake would lead to us gaining ten pounds, we'd probably never take it.

That leads me to the next issue we're faced with where comparison is concerned: too many options.

Take Aaron for example. Moses and Aaron had just led the nation of Israel out of captivity in Egypt. They stopped to camp at the bottom of Mount Sinai, and Moses went up to talk with God. Aaron was alone with the people at the bottom. Using Moses to deliver His words, the Lord devised the following plan with the Israelites: "*Now then, if you will indeed obey My voice and keep My covenant, then you shall be My own possession among all the peoples, for all the earth is Mine; and you shall be to Me a kingdom of priests and a holy nation*" (Exod. 19:5–6). The people agreed and said, "*All that the LORD has spoken we will do!*" (19:8). Moses climbed the mountain again to speak with God—where He gave him the Ten Commandments, ordinances of temple service, etc.—once more leaving Aaron to stay with the people. Everything was good, right? Keep reading.

The option God gave them through Moses was to wait until he returned (Exod. 24:14). But they got antsy. He was up there so long they didn't know what happened to him and got tired of waiting on him, so they thought of stuff to do on their own. They took all the gold they had, fashioned it into a golden calf, built an altar in front of it, threw a big party, presented a bunch of offerings on the altar, had a big meal together, and *"rose up to play"* (Exod. 32:1–6). Where did they come up with all that?

Have you ever heard The Living Bible 1971 translation of the verse: *"Idle hands are the devil's workshop; idle lips are his mouthpiece"* (Prov. 16:27)? It's like when your kids are playing in the other room, and it gets quiet, and you think, "Uh oh, what are they doing in there?" When we're bored, or just not intentional with our time, we tend to consider doing things we shouldn't.

What do you do when you're bored?

Here's what I'm getting at. If we allow the Bible to be our source of entertainment (and it's incredibly entertaining, y'all; there's scandal, murder, treason—you name it, it's in there), the enemy won't have an opportunity to introduce other options for consideration. But if we get bored with the Bible (because the world tells us it's old, outdated, and irrelevant), the enemy will use that to his advantage. He'll say, "Yeah, the Bible *is* outdated. Have you considered Facebook? What about Twitter, Instagram, Snapchat, Bumble, TikTok, and YouTube?" or any number of other things you could be doing? The next thing you know, you've spent hours/days/months in all that stuff and not one second in God's word.

If you took an inventory of your time for one week, how much time would you put down for social media?

TV?

Spending time in the Word?

In prayer?

Are you making Him a priority over all the other stuff?

The problem with too many options is that when we have several to choose from, we tend to crowd out the right, seemingly boring ones first. They keep getting overshadowed until they're no longer a possibility. That could happen with all good options too. What if a friend asks you to lead a life group on Sunday mornings after worship, lead a youth discipleship group, and help with the homeless on Tuesday nights? In addition to all that, you've got three kids, all of whom have different sports and activities they participate in, and you're the driver for them all. The point is that the world will *not* urge you toward God. It'll push you as far away as possible. We've got to be careful to make our time with the Lord a priority that won't get pushed to the back burner.

Do you have a set time for God? Is it a time that, come hell or high water, will happen? Or does it get crowded out by other stuff?

As we close today, take a moment to think of a time each day that you can spend with the Lord. If you're a morning person, it'd be best to do it in the morning. If you like to stay up late, do it then, after the kids are in bed. Try to make it a time you won't push. If you set it for an hour after work, you'll have to take somebody to a friend's house or cook dinner earlier because you've got people coming over. It needs to be a time that's consistently yours to spend as you see fit. If you don't have time that's consistently yours, think of ways to create some. Life does get busy, but we *make time* for what's important to us.

God, I pray for You to show us how crucial spending time with You is. Would You put it on our hearts to get to know You and fall in love with You daily? May we love time with You so much that we allow nothing to crowd it out. In Jesus's name, amen.

Day 5
Lust of the Eyes (Continued)

In the context of comparison, we sometimes draw conclusions or make assumptions. I heard a story about a church member who approached a preacher and asked him why he was mad at them. The preacher had no idea what they were talking about, so he asked. In response, the member went on to tell him that a few weeks back, when the pastor had just finished preaching, he walked past the person with a scowl on his face, and they just knew it was because they'd done something wrong.

The preacher explained he remembered that day because he'd eaten something new for breakfast, and it gave him terrible heartburn. After hearing the story, he was heartbroken. Not because that individual thought he was upset with them, but that they'd spent the last few weeks obsessing over what they could've done wrong when it had nothing at all to do with them.

Y'all, the enemy gets me here. I see people who are different from me, and I draw conclusions that may or may not have anything to do with their situation. It makes me see them from my perspective instead of the Lord's. From 1 Samuel 16:7b, one reads, "*For God sees not as man sees, for man looks at the outward appearance, but the LORD looks at the heart.*"

I'm not just talking about skin color either but about clothes, lifestyle, body type, etc. Society conditions us to make decisions about people based on external appearances. Let's play a game. I'm going to list the way some people look, and you write to the side what your first impression would be if you saw them on the street. Here goes.

- Girl in scrubs
- Really tall man
- Couple hugging
- Guy wearing overalls

That was a goofy exercise, but it makes you think. I'd probably assume the girl in scrubs is a nurse. I'd think the tall man plays basketball. I'd assume the couple hugging is a married couple meeting for lunch and the man wearing overalls is a farmer. My responses could be true, but they could also be inaccurate. The point is that we should look at the heart as God does.

Assuming we know something can also lead us to draw improper conclusions about who God is. Read John 21:18–23.

In this story, we see Peter comparing himself to John, the one whom Jesus loved. So, Peter, being Peter, says to Jesus, *"What about this man?"* (21:21). Jesus, knowing his heart, responds with, and I'm paraphrasing again: "If I want him to remain 'til I come back, what's it to ya?" (21:22).

Peter draws the conclusion from Jesus's response that John will live until Christ comes back, so he runs with it. He goes and tells his buddies the news.

Do you do that? Do you hear something from one person and run to tell everybody else?

Do you have to be the first to tell people things? If so, why?

Proverbs 10:19, *"When there are many words, transgression is unavoidable, but he who restrains his lips is wise,"* applies to the act of talking too much. I see people at work who'll only hear one side of a story or think they know all the details and tell everybody they see. The problem is they *don't* know the whole story, so when they spread the news company-wide, it starts a bunch of unnecessary drama. If they tell people incorrect information on a regular basis, they can become untrustworthy.

Many movements and theologies being taught today are riddled with error. They take a verse out of context, without taking it through sixty-six books of the Bible, draw improper conclusions about it, and build their entire doctrine around it, which is hazardous (Rev. 22:18–19). I believe this is why Paul tells us in 1 Thessalonians 5:17 to pray without ceasing. When we're in constant communication with the Lord, He can instruct our thinking, what we believe, and how to move forward in a way that's pleasing to Him.

Let's recap really quick before we move on and watch the progression unfold. In the context of comparison, we're considering options we shouldn't, wrong options drown out the right ones, and you've got to choose which way you're going to go.

That can lead us to make a rash decision just to find a moment of peace. Or we make the decision based on what the world would do instead of what God's word says about it. We become a follower, and the worst part about it is we don't even realize how dangerously appeasing society can be.

How do you make decisions? Do you Google it? Pray about it? Ask your friends?

As stated earlier, the enemy's goal is to keep us from spending time with God. When we're following the wrong thing or person, we're distracted and not considering what the Bible says. One example for us ladies is how we look. Girl, I'm stepping on some toes here—I know—but hear me out.

From 1 Peter 3:3–4, one reads: *"Let not your adornment be merely external—braiding the hair, and wearing gold jewelry, or putting on dresses; but let it be the hidden person of the heart, with the imperishable quality of a gentle and quiet spirit, which is precious in the sight of God."* We see all around us—on billboards, on TV, in movies and commercials—that we should look a certain way. We might assume that for people to love and accept us, we've got to be skinny, wear lots of makeup and jewelry, drive a certain kind of car, and have a big house. But remember, the world only considers the outer you.

God, however, looks at your heart. In the passage from 1 Peter, Peter isn't saying it's wrong to wear nice clothes, makeup, and jewelry. He's simply suggesting we focus more on the heart instead. The more outer stuff we put on, the more it can become a distraction—which, for some, is the point.

At the end of the comparison spiral is losing sight of reality and questioning everything you've known, or thought you knew, to be true. "Was what I learned in church growing up right? I've heard so many other ways of thinking. Which one is the truth? The world says it's okay to _____ (fill in the blank). Is it?"

In this day and time, do you know what's right and wrong?

What standard are you basing that on? The world's? The Bible's?

Where should we go for answers? God's word! The more time we spend there, the more He'll reveal things to us and begin to show us His view of topics like self-worth and identity. After all, God did create all things. Shouldn't we look to Him for answers anyway?

Y'all, comparison causes us to want what others have, to look like them, act like them, and do things like them. But God created us unique on purpose. He doesn't want a bunch of robots running around. He made each one of us the way we are for a specific reason. Nobody can say the things He has in store for you to say, the way you can say them. He uses our experiences, the good and the bad, to reach those who are going through something similar. If you don't believe me, read Romans 8:28.

God, this one is a tuffy for many women. Our eyes see several things about others that are intriguing. They look so different from us, and we see that as a bad thing most of the time. We may begin to put ourselves down, wish we looked like them, and begin the never-ending spiral of demeaning self-talk. Lord, use this study to teach us we don't have to stay there. Show us what life looks like through Your eyes. In Jesus's name, amen.

WEEK 2
Day 1
The Boastful Pride of Life

O ur topic for today is crucial, so we're going to camp out for a while.
You can define pride as consciousness of one's own worthiness or a feeling of deep pleasure or satisfaction derived from one's achievements. Being presumptuous, failing to observe the limits of what's permitted or appropriate, or being full of boldness are other forms of pride.

Whew! That was a mouthful, but what does it mean? Pride makes you draw attention to yourself. It leads you to talk about how great you are to others, even if they don't ask.

What are some things that come to mind when you think about pride?

Somebody at school or work who is arrogant. A parent talking endlessly about her kids. Is there a difference between pride and being proud? It's not a trick question, but think about it for a minute and write what you come up with below.

Let's see what the Bible says about pride.

- **Proverbs 16:5:** "*Everyone who is proud in heart is an abomination to the LORD; assuredly, he will not be unpunished.*"
- **Proverbs 26:12:** "*Do you see a man wise in his own eyes? There is more hope for a fool than for him.*"

- **Philippians 2:3:** *"Do nothing from selfishness or empty conceit, but with humility of mind let each of you regard one another as more important than himself."*
- **James 4:6:** *"But He gives a greater grace. Therefore, it says, 'GOD IS OPPOSED TO THE PROUD, BUT GIVES GRACE TO THE HUMBLE.'"*

These are just a few verses, but in this small sample, we can start to see that God dislikes pride. There are consequences for it. It can make you seem foolish and regard yourself higher than others. God is opposed to pride.

Read Daniel chapters 1–4. I know that's a long assignment, which is why it's pretty much the only thing we'll do for Day 1 this week.

I want you to get a picture in your mind about Nebuchadnezzar. Note anything to do with pride below.

God, I pray for You to give us eyes to see what You're Word is telling us about pride as we dig into Nebuchadnezzar. There's so much to learn in this rich text. May You speak Your truth in love. In Jesus's name, amen.

Day 2
Good ole Nebbie

In the book of Daniel, Nebuchadnezzar's reign was going well. Then he had a dream that he couldn't make heads or tails of. Daniel interpreted the vision and saved the lives of all the wise men in Babylon (Dan. 2:24, 47).

Can we pause for a second? Did you know that your obedience may affect many people? Something you do that you think is insignificant may save a whole generation of individuals. *Wow.*

Okay, back to the story. After hearing from Daniel, Nebuchadnezzar fell on his face, paid homage to Daniel, and said, *"Surely your God is a God of gods and a Lord of kings and a revealer of mysteries, since you have been able to reveal this mystery"* (2:47). Then he promoted Daniel to a higher position than all the wise men and gave his buddies more prestigious ranks than the administration.

I've read that before and thought the king was coming around. Not so, unfortunately. Keep reading.

Immediately following the promotions, Nebbie set up a golden image for people to bow to and worship at the call of music. If they didn't worship the golden idol, the king's men would throw them into a furnace of blazing fire. Wait a minute now. He was just talking about Daniel's God being the God of gods, so why would he want everybody to worship some silly statue?

Why do we encourage others to binge-watch the same shows as us?

Why do we make time for anything and everything besides the God we claim to know and love?

People loyal to the king found Daniel's friends not worshiping as instructed and threw them into the fire.

Which would you rather do: Obey the law established by man so you don't get tossed into the fiery furnace? Or live by God's word and accept the consequences of your actions?

Have you had to make a decision like that before? If so, record it below and think about sharing with the group.

Daniel's buddies chose to stand on God's word. And guess what? God protected them! So much so that the flames had no effect on them. In fact, when they came out of the fire, the intense heat had neither singed a hair on their head nor damaged their trousers. The smell of fire hadn't even come upon them (Dan. 3:27).

Something interesting to note is that the Lord saved Shadrach, Meshach, and Abednego (the prophet's friends) from the fire, but look at what the three men said prior to entering the furnace. Read Daniel 3:16–18.

In answer to the question of what god could save them if they were thrown into the fire, they said, and I'm still paraphrasing, "We don't have to answer your question, and we know that our God is able to save us, but even if He doesn't, we're *still* not going to serve your gods or worship the golden image." Man, that's bold.

It's easy to see their obedience paid off because God preserved them from the fire. However, if we didn't see them saved, would their deaths still be an example we should follow? In other words, when we're faced with a decision to compromise or stand firm, will we be able to endure even if He doesn't deliver us?

I mean, think about these guys. They were within a fire that was so hot it killed the people who delivered them to it. Nobody could see a way out for them—the three men included—but they were okay with it because they trusted God.

Do you trust Him that much? Or do you just talk about trusting Him, but when faced with a tough decision, you compromise?

Daniel's God amazed Nebbie so much he issued a decree that if anybody said anything offensive about the God of these boys, they'd be torn limb from limb and their houses reduced to rubbish (Dan. 3:29). Now the king is making progress, right? Keep reading.

JLT #4—Have you ever found yourself reading a verse of scripture but not understanding what it's talking about? I'd encourage you to read the verses that come before it and the ones after. Often, scripture will explain itself if you give it enough time.

Looking over the surrounding verses gives you more context that can help explain what's happening.

The king had another dream about a great tree, but this time, the vision wasn't so good for him. Daniel explained that he'd be driven away from mankind, dwell in the fields with the beasts for years, come to his senses, recognize that the Most High is ruler over humanity, and after that, the Lord would restore his kingdom (Dan. 4:4–27).

Daniel's interpretation freaked Nebuchadnezzar out, but days/weeks/months went by, and nothing happened. Twelve months later, he was walking on the roof of the royal palace of Babylon, thinking to himself, "*Is this not Babylon the great, which I myself have built as a royal residence by the might of my power and for the glory of my majesty?*" (4:30). That's pride, y'all. But before he could finish his sentence, Daniel's words came true. God sent the king out to graze on grass like the beasts of the field. Then, when he came to his senses and gave glory to God, he returned to his reign (4:28–33).

He looked around, saw how awesome the kingdom was, and mentally patted himself on the back. The king really thought he had something to do with all his success. All throughout Nebuchadnezzar's story, he acknowledged God, but only after he got what he wanted. Pride deceives you into thinking you dictate your success.

Do you only recognize God when something miraculous happens, or do you only recognize Him when you need something?

As we close today, take inventory of your time with God. I'll close us in prayer, but if you have the ability, spend a little more time praying to Him for yourself. Maybe ask Him to show you the pride in your life.

God, I come to You today with a heavy heart. Pride kills. It takes our eyes off You and puts them on ourselves. Father, You made us. You know our tendencies—where we're strong and where we're weak. Protect us from flawed thinking that leads to pride. Help us to humble ourselves at your feet daily. In Jesus's name, amen.

Day 3
Insecurity

Looking at your accomplishments isn't the only way pride can hurt you. Did you know that insecurity can be a form of pride? I read an article that said, "'What will they think of me?' That is the question insecure people ask themselves. I ask, 'What makes you believe people are thinking about you?'"[3] The quote brings up a good point. Not only do we pridefully assume others are often thinking about us, but we frequently give in to the need to be judged positively.

We diet so we'll look good. We get our hair, nails, and toes done to draw attention to how pretty we can be. We buy lots of makeup so people won't see our flaws. Our flaws become an obsession that gets worse the longer we dwell on them. Why do we do that? Would it be so bad if I went to the grocery store without makeup on? What about my face is so awful that it would make everybody run, screaming in terror, like I was Godzilla? I know that sounds silly, but that's how it seems sometimes in my mind.

> **JLT #5**—According to a 2017 study OnePoll did for Groupon, the average woman spends $313 per month on her appearance. That adds up to $3,756 per year and $225,360 over a lifetime. Men spend slightly less at $244 per month.[4] And for what? Imagine what good we could do with all that money instead. Can we consider these numbers for a minute? If you want a real gut punch, monitor your spending for one month on things you do to "better" your appearance.

---

[3] Dave Anderson, "Pride and Insecurity are Linked," Anderson Leadership Solutions, June 6, 2017, http://www.andersonleadershipsolutions.com/pride-insecurity/.

[4] Chelsea Haynes, "True Cost of Beauty: Survey Reveals Where Americans Spend Most," Groupon Merchant, August 3, 2017, https://www.groupon.com/merchant/trends-insights/market-research/true-cost-beauty-americans-spend-most-survey.

I have a big forehead, my eyes are close together so that when I don't wear makeup people think I'm cross-eyed, and I sweat in places I don't think ladies should. There! The cat is outta the bag. Those aren't all of my "flaws," but it sure feels good to get them off my chest. That's the thing with insecurity: once you profess it, and people know about it, you don't have to hide it anymore.

What are some things you try to hide from others?

Does your desire to hide your flaws consume your thoughts, time, or money?

The good news is that when you go to God with your insecurities and ask Him to show you what to do about them, He will. As I began to spend more and more time with the Father, He began to reveal who I was in Him.

Look up the following verses and match them with the correct description of you when you're placed into Christ:

1. 2 Corinthians 5:21   Our citizenship is in heaven
2. 1 Peter 1:5   Called, beloved in God, kept for Jesus
3. Colossians 1:22   Protected by the power of God
4. Philippians 3:20   Holy, blameless, beyond reproach
5. Romans 5:1   Sealed with the Holy Spirit of promise
6. Jude 1:1   Justified by faith, at peace with God through Jesus
7. Ephesians 1:13   We're the righteousness of God in Him

These are just a few verses, but I hope you see how special you are to God. As we reviewed earlier, He looks at the heart and not our outer appearance (1 Samuel 16:7b).

Jackie, the Bible teacher who taught us about spiritual maturity (the same guy I mentioned in the introduction), taught a class on the book of Romans. It was during that study that God began to show me my true identity in Him. When you're a new believer, or just haven't matured much spiritually, it may not be easy to believe positive things about yourself. If you're like me, the enemy has filled your head with lies for so long you have to unlearn a lot to move forward.

What are some lies you believe about yourself?

What's your typical response when you think of them?

The devil would tell me things like, "You say you believe in God, but you party every night," or "That guy dumped you because you were fat. Why would anybody else want you?" or my favorite, "Why would anybody believe what you say about God? Look at your past!" I used to actually think these thoughts. They're so convincing, and most of the time, there's a little bit of truth sprinkled in them.

The one thing the enemy hopes you don't realize is that once you accept life in Christ, God casts our sins as far as the east is from the west (Ps. 103:12), is merciful to our iniquities, and will remember our sins no more (Heb. 8:12).

Satan is freaking out right now! He's terrified that if you dig out this truth for yourself, start living by it, and replace his lies with God's word, you'll learn to overcome him. Defying the devil is what it means to become a "young man" like we talked about earlier in 1 John 2.

It sounds easy, right? *Wrong.* The longer we stay in our insecurity, the more habits or default settings we create. The longer we drill those default settings into our brains, the harder it is to change them.

What do you need to do to get those thoughts out of your head?

Well, the good news is that we're not the ones responsible for changing them. In fact, if we try with our own power to adjust our ways of living, we may succeed for a little while, but it won't last. We'll end up frustrated and defeated, which is exactly what Satan wants.

In 2 Corinthians 3:18, one reads, *"But we all, with unveiled face beholding as in a mirror the glory of the Lord, are being transformed into the same image from glory to glory, just as from the Lord, the Spirit."*

As we spend time with God, in His word, beholding Him as in a mirror, He begins to change us. That transformation continues while we walk with Him. People we encounter will start to see more of Him through us.

Are you spending time in the Word?

How much?

What's your reason for reading the Bible? To memorize verses? So you can speak intelligently about it? So you can teach it?

Those are all good reasons for reading the Bible, but they shouldn't be the main purpose. We talk to God through prayer. God speaks to us through His word. We shouldn't go to the Bible for what we get out of it but for what He gets out of it. God desires a relationship with us. If our focus is on getting to know the God who wrote this love letter to us, He'll begin to honor that time by changing us into His image. If we had another month or so, I'd tell you all the changes the Lord made in my life, but that's a story for another time. I'll say that allowing Him to change you is a process. Spiritual growth doesn't happen overnight. God isn't a fast-food chain that's there to serve you quickly. He wants your time, your focus, and your heart.

The following example is a little off topic from pride, but it's relevant because it concerns how and with whom you spend your time. A dear friend of mine used to tell her kids, "Show me your friends, and I'll show you your future." She was trying to get them to understand that who they hung around mattered. Proverbs 13:20 says, *"He who walks with wise men will be wise, but the companion of fools will suffer harm."*

You know when you walk into a Subway restaurant, no matter how long you're in there, you leave smelling like it. The people your kids spend time with will impact them! If you notice your child acting differently, it's most likely because they've made a new friend. A lot of times, you've done nothing unusual in the way you parent. Rather, the difference in their behavior is because they're listening to someone else. The "friend" is introducing your child to some of those options they didn't know they had.

Address it, y'all. Ask questions, and I mean good, open-ended questions that will draw out some discussion. No yes-or-no stuff here. The positive and negative impacts new friends can have on your kids are too meaningful to ignore.

Who we hang around will affect our lives, for better or worse. The more time we spend with God, allowing Him to teach us straight from His heart to ours, the more He'll change our behaviors to align with His. Unfortunately, the more time we spend with the world, the more we look, act, and talk like it.

God, we learn with difficulty and forget with ease. May You teach us as we sit with You—first that we have the freedom to fail, and second that when we do fail, we can run to You. You love us so much. May You show us when we're off track. May You give us a Nathan to call us out when we can't see our faults. Let Your opinion be the one we care about most. In Jesus's name, amen.

Day 4
Work, Work, Work

Another way that pride plays a role in distracting us from Him is through our work. The world defines success by the things you have, the status you've achieved, and how recognizable you are. Well, one way to get all those things is to become great at work.

Read Luke 22:24–27 and note what you see.

Even Jesus's disciples wanted to be the greatest. The Twelve argued about it. Jesus told them to let the greatest become as the least and the leader the servant.

God created work to be a joyful experience of liberation. People should do it for His glory as we saw with Adam in the garden (Gen. 2:15). So, where did we get the idea of climbing the corporate ladder? You guessed it. Your boy Satan. He's so clever, isn't he?

Our world is saturated with people who are trying to "make it" one way or the other. Parents want their kids to be famous. Or they want them to be doctors, lawyers, or owners of companies. Don't hear what I'm not saying either. I'm not saying there's anything wrong with any of the occupations I've listed. Wanting to be the best at what you do is fine…unless your motivation is for what *you* get out of it. That's where we go wrong. And that pride doesn't only apply to work. It could have to do with your child's sports, after-school activities, popularity, etc.

For example, your son makes it on the rec league baseball team. He works hard and likes it a lot, so you start to push him a little harder. He sees that when he does good in baseball it makes you happy, so he keeps applying himself. As your kid grows up, he keeps excelling. High school coaches eventually notice and ask him to try out for varsity. He makes the team and is a starter. Next thing you know, you're going on recruiting visits to colleges around the country. The young man gets a full ride to a competitive university, and after helping his team to a successful season, the big-league scouts are calling. They draft him, and you think to yourself, "We made it!"

That's great, but does he know Jesus as his Lord and Savior? Not to be too pessimistic, but the world is so good at distracting us with material things that we forget our lives are temporary. Things of the world will pass away. Eternal things, like heaven and hell, last forever.

Don't fall for it, ladies. Some of you may come from a legalistic family that said women stay home and raise babies. Now that you're out on your own, you can work if you want to. And not only that, but you're also going to be great at whatever job you get. I hope you see that I'm not against a woman in the workplace given I myself work. I'm trying to get you to understand that the world (and the enemy driving it all) is full of *deception*.

Let's say you climb to the top of the corporate ladder and become the president or owner. You started as a part-time admin and have worked, clawed, and scratched your way to the top. Congrats! But I have some questions. Did you compromise to get there? Did you do things you wouldn't normally do to make it to the next level? Did you hurt someone in the process?

Again, I'm not saying that women shouldn't be presidents or owners. I'm simply trying to get you to see that our motivations should be eternal. God can certainly use us women, and our success in the workplace, to accomplish His work. But it should be His work through us. We must stand on His word throughout our professional lives. If we're presented with something a little shady or a way to cut corners to get ahead faster, we should say no. But if we deny opportunities, our superiors might pass us over for a promotion or, worse, fire us. So what? God's plan is the best one for you anyway.

Have you experienced anything like that in your life?

Have you been forced to make a tough decision at work? You knew the way you wanted to go was wrong, but it would mean getting ahead. Did you do it anyway?

When I think of people in the Bible who stood on God's word even when nobody stood with them, I think of Joseph. He was his father's favorite and flaunted that fact. His brothers hated him for it, enough to want to kill him, but they sold him into slavery instead (Gen. 37:25–28). Traders took him to Egypt, where he eventually became the master of the house of Potiphar, an Egyptian officer to Pharaoh (Gen. 39:1–6). It sounds like he got through the struggle and achieved success, right? Keep reading.

Potiphar's wife liked the way Joseph looked and asked him to be with her. He refused, to the point of fleeing naked when she pulled his garments and wouldn't let go. She lied to her husband about what happened. She said Joseph came on to her and wouldn't take no for an answer, so Potiphar had him thrown into prison (39:19–23).

Has anyone falsely accused you?

How did you handle it?

I think it's important to stop here for a second and notice what we *don't* read. Joseph isn't asking for a different judge. He's not asking for the security camera footage to prove his innocence. There's no record in this account of him pleading his case at all. He simply trusts that God will work out the details.

Y'all, pride and indignation can trick us. When somebody does me wrong, I have the uncontrollable urge to plead my case. I want people to know what *really* happened. I want them to know that the other person is really at fault, not me. I want the truth to come out so my name is cleared.

Have you noticed anything about the previous paragraph? It's all about me! None of it points to Him.

Is your life all about you? Take a few minutes to explain why or why not. God, take this time to give us clarity about ourselves. Open our eyes to see.

If you keep reading the story of Joseph, you'll see he interpreted Pharaoh's dream, got promoted to second in command under Pharaoh, and ended up saving the world from famine (Gen. 40 and 50).

If he would've complained about going to prison, he may not have been in prison with the cupbearer and baker to hear about their dreams. He may not have been there to interpret the visions for them, and in turn, the cupbearer may not have told Pharaoh that he met a guy in prison who could tell him the meaning of his dreams.

Joseph trusted God. He went along in life, standing on His word. He didn't worry about defending himself. The Bible tells us not to take our revenge. Rather, we should leave room for God's wrath, as it's written, " '*VENGEANCE IS MINE, I WILL REPAY,' says the Lord. 'BUT IF YOUR ENEMY IS HUNGRY, FEED HIM, AND IF HE IS THIRSTY, GIVE HIM A DRINK; FOR IN SO DOING YOU WILL HEAP BURNING COALS UPON HIS HEAD.' Do not be overcome by evil, but overcome evil with good*" (Rom. 12:19–21).

I'm not sure how Joseph knew all that, but he did. Genesis 50:20 says, "*As for you, you meant evil against me,* but *God meant it for good in order to bring about this present result.*" If Joseph had been focused on himself instead of doing God's will, his story would likely have turned out differently. Yes, he suffered trials along the way (being sold into slavery, falsely accused, and thrown into prison), but he wasn't worried about himself. God's purpose for his life was more important than his success.

Oh God, may You show us how to get there! In Jesus's name, amen!

Let's talk more about work. Look up the following verses and write what the Bible says about it: Colossians 3:23, Proverbs 16:3, 1 Corinthians 10:31, Ephesians 4:28, and 2 Thessalonians 3:10.

These verses are a little scattered, but they all point to one thing. *It's not about you.* The scripture passages tell us that we should do work for one of two reasons:

- For God's glory
- To help others

Nowhere in these verses does it mention getting to the top of the corporate ladder.

I heard a friend telling a story about a great movie he watched. *King Richard* is about Venus and Serena Williams, whose dad pushed them to focus on their education first. School comes before practice, before games, before tournaments. The film emphasized the mindset that your education comes first because it will make you stand out. Sports will fade away, your body will fail, but your education will sustain you.

Do you see anything wrong with that philosophy?

I mean, the dad is correct. Our bodies will fail us eventually, but his stance broke my heart a little. There were about six of us sitting around the table listening to the story, and everybody was so intrigued and pleased that Mr. Williams had pushed his daughters to pursue education over sports.

All I could think was, "But do they know Jesus?"

Status symbols don't matter when you die. Degrees, promotions, and sports are temporary things you have on earth. When you pass on and go to eternity, those things don't travel with you. The father spent his girls' entire life focusing on things that only matter down here.

When you're standing before the Father, He's not going to look at you and say, "Well now, I see that you won gold in the Olympics, so come on in," or "I understand that you graduated summa cum laude from the Harvard doctorate program in science. Get in here, Dr. Smith."

You may feel like I'm belaboring the point, but it's biblical. Near the end of the Sermon on the Mount, Jesus talks about people who *claim* to know Him but don't. Jesus will tell those individuals to depart from Him. *Yikes.* He also said in that part of the sermon that people will know Christians by their fruit.

What fruit is your tree producing? Good work, lots of money, fame, and material possessions?

Or are you producing fruit that'll lead others to Him?

One more thing before we move on. Like the father mentioned in today's lesson, wanting his kids to be famous athletes, we also want people to know us. To be educated or famous, you may be tempted to make that your life. You eat, sleep, and breathe it 'til you achieve it, right?

What's your driving force?

What motivates you to go all in at work? The gym? The PTA (is that still a thing)?

The issue with staying too focused on the grind is that when you make something your life, it can become your identity. And when you lose it, you're lost. When famous athletes retire, they're often left empty. They're not in the spotlight anymore, and they don't know how to deal with it.

When you make something other than God your life, it's difficult to maintain. Like the famous athletes above, eventually our bodies give out, and we can't sustain the effort of the game anymore. But whatever "it" is that we've built our life upon is from the fallen world. Things down here will disappoint you, people included.

Read the following verses, and record what the Bible tells us about God. Joshua 1:5, Psalm 118:6, Malachi 3:6, Romans 8:31, and John 16:33.

I hope these passages will encourage you to make Him your life instead of anything temporal. I'm paraphrasing again, but hopefully you'll see that God is worth it.

No man will stand before you. I will be with you, and I will never leave you or forsake you (Josh. 1:5). He is for me; I will not fear. What can man do? (Ps. 118:6). I (God) do not change (Mal. 3:6). If God is for us, who can be against us? (Rom. 8:31). You'll have trouble in the world but take comfort. I've overcome the world (John 16:33).

God is the only One who won't fail us.

God, I come to You with praise today. Thank You for never letting me down! Thank You for waiting patiently for me to get over myself and seek You. Thank You for teaching me when I sit at Your feet and give You time to change me. I love You so much. In Jesus's name, amen.

Day 5
The World

As stated earlier, there are three avenues that tempt us: the world, the flesh, and the devil. We've already talked about the flesh and the devil, but let's spend more time on the world.

The world tells us life is all about us. God's word tells us the exact opposite. Matthew 6:33 says, *"But seek first His kingdom and His righteousness; and all these things shall be added to you."* His word tells us to focus on Him first, not on being the smartest, the best, or most famous. We should seek the Lord! Once we know Him and His righteousness, He'll give us *"all these things."*

If you look back a little in Matthew 6, the "all these things" isn't talking about our deepest desires. It's talking about how He provides food for the birds (verse 26) and beauty for the lilies of the field (verses 27–29) even though they don't work for it.

This verse isn't telling us that if we seek Him, He'll give us a winning lottery ticket. God will provide the things we *need*. The more we seek the Father, the more He'll change our desires to line up with His. We'll care less and less about what the world thinks we should wear, accomplish at work, spend our time doing…and the list goes on.

The message in Matthew 6 is about the motives of our hearts. Jesus talks about doing things, godly things, to attract attention. The listener's *motives* were the issue, not their actions. They were giving publicly so everybody would see and be impressed. They were reciting prayers in the squares so all would hear how spiritual they were.

JLT #6—Jesus tells them right before the Lord's Prayer not to pray like the Gentiles, who by meaningless repetition suppose their prayers will be heard, or the hypocrites, who stand in the synagogues and on street corners for men to see and hear them. What if the "Lord's Prayer" isn't supposed to be recited as such? Have you ever considered instead that He gave it as a format for how they should structure prayer? It starts with praise and submission (verses 9–10), supplication and confession are next (verses 11–

12), and finally protection and praise (verse 13). If you have extra time, you can read Exodus 25–31 and 35–40. Those chapters give details about the temple the way God intended it to be. The structure for the Lord's Prayer lines up perfectly with the furniture of the temple and their purpose.

The end of Matthew 6:5 sums up why we shouldn't aspire to conform: *"Truly, I say to you, they have their reward in full."* Doing things for attention and fame gets us attention and fame, and that's it. In other words, when we do things for the world to recognize us, it might, but that will be our *only* reward. This world will be the best we'll get for our efforts. Isn't that a scary thought? My statement on page 8 was, "There's got to be more than this!"

If life on earth was all you got, would you be okay with it?

We can also get caught up in materialism if our focus is on the things of the world. Look up these verses and write what you see about material possessions: Matthew 6:21, 24, Ecclesiastes 5:10, 1 Timothy 6:10, and Hebrews 13:5.

The Bible is clear about what loving things from this fallen world will bring. Galatians 6:7 says, *"Do not be deceived, God is not mocked; for whatever a man sows, this he will also reap."* That's true on either side of the coin. If you put your focus on things of the world, you'll reap things of the world. If you focus on eternal things, you'll reap eternal rewards.

Read Romans 8. Fill out the chart below with fruit you get when you're in the flesh and in the spirit. I'll give you the first couple. There may be more than you have room to record.

In The Flesh (temporary)	In The Spirit (eternal)
Sin condemned in the flesh	There's no condemnation for those in Christ
The mind set on the flesh is death	The mind set on the spirit is life and peace

Let's take this thought a little deeper. Romans 1:18 says, *"For the wrath of God is revealed from heaven against all ungodliness and unrighteousness of men, who suppress the truth in unrighteousness."*

When we're focused on things of the world, or have our mind set on the flesh, we can begin suppressing the truth in unrighteousness. Once you bury the truth, you'll see that your thoughts and actions don't provoke God's will for your life.

Can you tell when you're suppressing truth?

If so, what's it look like? Excuses? Anxiety? Busyness? Fear?

Our world is fallen; it breeds insecurity, lust, and selfishness and brings you to a place of emptiness where you'll constantly try to fill the void with stuff. That stuff won't satisfy you. It'll just leave you wanting more.

Eternal things like God's word, an intimate relationship with our Creator, and spending time alone with Him will bring you peace in the craziness of everyday life.

So, what happens if we *do* focus on the world? What happens if we crave fame and let it guide us for a season?

God, I come to You brokenhearted because pride is rampant in a world that's constantly telling us to get more stuff because "we're worth it." That slogan in itself is not the problem. Thinking we deserve more stuff because of something we've done or have is the issue. If we're worth anything, it's because of You. Down here, pride will lead us away from You and will encourage us to seek our reward from society. We may end up there for a time, but may we never stay there! God, may You show us that today. In Jesus's name, amen.

WEEK 3
Day 1
Motives and Perspective

Ephesians 2:3 says, *"Among them we too all formerly lived in the lusts of our flesh, indulging the desires of the flesh and of the mind, and were by nature children of wrath, even as the rest."* It reads, "formerly lived" and "were by nature children of wrath."

Look up Colossians 2:13, Romans 5:8, and Romans 5:10 and write below what else we *were*.

We were dead in our transgressions, sinners, and enemies of God.

What's my point?

First, we, as members of the body, are supposed to be different from those who aren't members.

Second, we're supposed to be more different today than we were yesterday.

Those who aren't members are indulging the lusts of their flesh and most likely only looking to meet their needs—floundering through life without an eternal purpose. We aren't. We're part of a new family with a specific calling within the body of Christ. The "church" is the body of Christ.

Look up the following verses and write what being "the body of Christ" means.

Romans 12:5, 1 Corinthians 12:12–27, Ephesians 3:6, and Ephesians 4:15–16.

Once we're members of the body, we must support each other, help each other grow, and understand that we, no matter how small or seemingly insignificant a part we are, are necessary to the body's overall growth and well-being. Did you get that? *No matter how small or seemingly insignificant a part of the body we are, we are necessary.* God has a specific plan for each of us.

Why do you think God gives each of His children a special purpose only they can accomplish?

I believe it's because nobody else will be able to perform your duty the way you will. For example, there are many great gymnasts in the world—some of them outstanding—but none of them, in their own bodies, can ever do what Simone Biles does with hers.

The enemy does a good job of keeping us from being different. That bondage keeps us isolated, which is contrary to the biblical way of life described in the previously mentioned verses.

So, what's keeping you from being the part of the body it needs you to be? Amazon Prime? Hulu? YouTube TV? Facebook, Twitter, Snapchat, or Instagram?

Do you think you need to be like somebody else (another part of the body) to fit in?

Why?

The world tells us we should be our own person. "You do you, boo," right? But in the same breath, through advertisements, Hollywood movies, news media, and trends, it says we should look the same, act the same, dress the same, talk the same, and raise our kids the same as everybody else does. So, which is it?

God's word provides a contrast of how the *world* acts versus how *we* should act. Read Galatians 5:19–21 and note the deeds of the flesh (how the world acts) below.

Looking up these words in Greek (you can Google it) can shed some light on them and give you some richness to the meaning of each one.

Do any of these behaviors point others to Christ?

Now, read Galatians 5:22–23 and note the fruit of the Spirit (how we're supposed to act).

God didn't intend to have a bunch of robots walking around that all look like Barbie dolls. He created us each with our own unique qualities, as stated above, specifically designed to build up the body of Christ. The Lord calls us, as Christians, to be different from this world (Rom. 12:2), yet we spend our lives trying to fit in with it. I was watching a Hallmark movie recently; it was a Cinderella-type story for Christmas. The girl went to the gala in somebody else's place and was "just trying to fit in." Prince Charming told her that if she would have fit in, she'd have never stood out to him. That's the point. If we conform to the world, we won't stand out the way God intended.

One of our goals in life should be to be more spiritually mature tomorrow than we are today and to finish better than we started (2 Tim. 4:7–8). The first person who comes to mind when I think of somebody finishing better than they started is Paul.

Read Acts 8:1–3 and 9:1–9.

Paul was persecuting Christians, throwing them in prison, and trying to get them killed. He was zealous for Judaism and wanted anybody who believed differently to suffer the consequences. Followers of Jesus knew him for doing much harm to the saints (9:13–14), so much so that after God converted Paul, the disciples were afraid to believe he was truly on their side (9:26). But since God is known to do a lot with a little, He said in 9:15, *"Go, for he is a chosen instrument of Mine, to bear My name before the Gentiles and kings and the sons of Israel."* God changed him 180 degrees and can do the same with us.

How quickly the transformation happens is up to you and me. Paul's conversion was pretty fast. I believe that to be true for two reasons. First, because according to Acts 22:14, he was *"appointed...to know His will, and to see the Righteous One, and to hear an utterance from His mouth,"* and second, because he was willing.

There are many people out there who'll teach and preach that individuals like Paul and other leaders in the Bible didn't have a choice, that the Lord irresistibly drew them to where they couldn't refuse. I believe they could, in fact, refuse if they wanted to. Take Jonah for example. God called him to go and prophesy to Nineveh (Jon. 1:2), but instead, he fled in the opposite direction, going to Tarshish to run from the presence of the Lord (1:3).

Has God ever called you to do something that scared you or, like Jonah, made you mad?

For most people who come to the Lord, it seems they take years to see change. I know that's true in my life, but I don't think it's because God was slacking. It's because I wanted to have my cake and eat it too. I wanted to go to church on Sunday and be spiritual, sing the hymns, and put money in the plate to feel recharged and ready to go, only to look, act, and talk like the rest of the world for the rest of the week.

Think about it in terms of exercising. What if you wanted to look like a bodybuilder, but you only worked out one day a week? How long do you think that limited routine would take to transform your body?

Moses's adoptive parents raised him in the Egyptian culture, but he knew the Israelites were his brothers. He went out to visit them one day when he was around forty (Acts 7:23) and saw an Egyptian beating one of his brothers. He killed the Egyptian and buried him in the sand. He thought his brethren (the Israelites) understood that God was granting them deliverance through him (7:25). So, when he went to visit them again the next day, he saw two of his brothers fighting and attempted to separate them. They called him out for killing the Egyptian the day before and asked who put him in charge, so he fled to Midian. He stayed there for forty years (Acts 7:26–30).

God's timing is perfect, and I believe it has a lot to do with Him knowing our spiritual maturity. He's not going to give us something we're not ready to handle. Like I was saying earlier, He doesn't want a bunch of robots roaming around simply doing what they were programmed to do. God made us unique. He'll give us as much of Him as we want. We just have to choose to seek Him. He won't force Himself on us.

Back to Paul. I'm sure you know his story, but in case you don't, he was beaten, left for dead, shipwrecked, and thrown in prison for the rest of his life on account of Christ.

How do you think he felt about all that? Read 2 Corinthians 4:16–17.

He considered it "momentary light affliction." Can you believe that? I don't know about you, but if somebody beat me up, threw me in prison, and left me for dead, I'd probably have a hard time saying, "Eh…it'll be all right." I'd like to think I could, but when you're going through difficult times, it's hard to keep an eternal perspective.

Paul's own conclusion of his life was written to his "true child in the faith" (1 Tim. 1:2) in 2 Timothy 4:7–8. Take a minute or two to read through it and record what you see.

It's truly inspiring. Even at the end of his life, Paul spends more time talking about the future ("*There is laid up for me the crown of righteousness, which the Lord…will award to me,*" 4:8) and others ("*and not only to me but also to all who have loved His appearing,*" 4:8). He understood the temporary nature of life on earth. I think that's why he considered his affliction momentary. He didn't waste time scrolling through Instagram or Snapchat. Yeah, I know they weren't around back then, but I believe if they were, he wouldn't have wasted his time with 'em. Paul knew his time was best spent with others, talking about God and His free gift of salvation. He devoted his life to reaching others for Christ but not because God forced him to. He chose to forsake all else and follow the Lord just like the disciples in Jesus's day (Luke 5:11).

If a faith-based life is that easy, why doesn't everybody have one?

Good question. Staying focused on Him is hard work. I'll give you an example. I used to coach gymnastics, and I worked for a gym whose gymnasts constantly took first place in individual and team competitions but especially excelled in the uneven parallel bars. The owner was meticulous in his methods. He spent years developing a system that would train his athletes to be prepared mentally and physically and also to peak at the right time. He had coaches coming up to him frequently, asking how year after year he accomplished so much.

He finally held a bars clinic to teach the coaches in the area—his direct competition—how he ran his workouts. He gave them his conditioning plans, his progressions, his weekly workouts, and how long it would take for a gymnast to master each skill. He was an open book! He told them exactly what he did to win. They had the exact same information he used, but do you think anything changed? Nope. Information is just information until you put it into practice. Doing the workouts like he planned was demanding, tedious, and required great effort. Even though the other coaches knew what they'd get out of it if they followed his plan, putting in that kind of effort *still* wasn't worth it to them.

I think about that story all the time. There were consistently twenty people who heard the same teaching as me and my husband during our church's Bible studies. However, the majority made it through the courses and went right on living their lives just like they did before. There were only a few of us who were ignited into a new way of life. I ask God in my prayers, "Why me? Why did You teach us these things, but people who heard the exact same teaching we did didn't get it?" I'm convinced it's because we had willing hearts to receive His word. That's been my prayer for you throughout the writing process, that you'll have a willing heart and desire to know Him intimately.

Our walk with God is no cakewalk either. We have all the information we need (the Bible), and we have the mind of Christ (1 Cor. 2:16), but that doesn't mean we can walk the earth sinless and free. We have to *choose* to turn our backs on the world and seek Him. That sounds simple, right? It's not. But the more time I spend alone with the Lord, the easier it gets. He shows me little by little, as I allow Him, how to overcome the enemy's temptations.

God, our world is in such a hurry. I get caught up in the hustle-bustle all the time. I'm one of the least patient people I know, but You're never in a hurry. You're never early or late. Your timing is perfect. May You teach us to wait. May You show us that You have our best interest in mind, and just because You don't answer us right away doesn't mean the answer is no. May You enlighten us to Your process so we can learn to appreciate the time it takes to complete it. In Jesus's name, amen!

Day 2
And Now We Fight (Starting with Prayer)

P aul tells us in his letter to the Ephesians how he was able to walk with the Lord. He spells out exactly what armor we have, its purpose in our lives, and how we are to use it. Read Ephesians 6:10–20 and make a note of the six pieces of armor below.

But before we get into the actual pieces of armor, we've got to know why Paul mentions them. Read Ephesians 6:11–13 again and note who our battle is with and how we're supposed to fight it.

The first thing Paul tells his readers is to be strong in the Lord. Let's stop there for just a minute. He didn't say work your butt off, do whatever you can on your own, then get all your buddies together to fight. No. He told them to be strong *in the Lord*. If you keep reading, you'll see why.

In Ephesians 6:12, it states that *"our struggle is not against flesh and blood, but against the rulers, against the powers, against the world forces of this darkness, against the spiritual* forces *of wickedness in the heavenly places."*

So, we're not fighting flesh and blood. Wait…does that mean when somebody says something about us, we're not supposed to fight back? Yep. You shouldn't, unless what you say will glorify God (and I've not found any of my sassy comebacks pointing anybody to Him). Y'all, verse 12 is not a popular message, but it's true. Everything about the world teaches us to defend ourselves or prove ourselves and our worth. It's not *who* you are that matters. It's *whose* you are.

Think back to Joseph. Did he plead his case or spend all his money on the best attorney so everybody would know he was innocent? Nope. He spoke when the situation moved him to speak and stayed quiet when it didn't. Our struggle is spiritual. Satan accuses us to God (Job 1:6–12 and 2:1–6), and his pawns attack whoever he tells them to.

JLT #7—That's some deep stuff, y'all. I'm not going to dwell on spiritual battles long because I don't fully understand them all yet, but I do think that when we pray, it activates angels to fight for us in heaven (Heb. 1:14). The more we pray, the more strength they receive. Read Daniel 10, focusing on verses 12–14. I know it's long, but our lesson for this week is short, so spend some time on the passage if you can. Daniel was praying, and the angel heard him and was planning to come but was held up for three weeks. Just some food for thought.

Before we close for the day and move on to the actual pieces of armor, let's see if we can find the glue that holds our defenses together. Read Ephesians 6:18–20 and see if you can recognize it.

Prayer! We are to pray at all times in the Spirit, petitioning and staying alert with perseverance for all the saints.

Look up these verses and find out what else the Bible says about prayer: Philippians 4:6–7, 1 Thessalonians 5:17, James 5:16, Jeremiah 33:3, and Matthew 26:41.

God desires for us to run to Him with anything and everything. When you drop the ball, do you run to Him? Why or why not?

Guess what? He knows what you're thinking anyway, so you might as well go ahead and talk it out. The quote from 1 Thessalonians 5:17 says to *"pray without ceasing."* Does that mean we're to sit in the closet all day with our eyes closed and heads bowed? I suppose you could, but that's not practical, is it? I think it means to keep the dialogue open throughout the day. I've noticed that the more time I spend in prayer, the more I catch the sassy words before they make it out of my mouth. Y'all, that's a big step for me. I have a big fat mouth, and I'm not afraid to use it. The more I run things through my "God" filter, the less I say that leads others away from Him.

God, You gave holy armor to Paul to share not only with his readers at the time but also with us. May we take Your gift seriously. May we start each day

with You in prayer, putting on the armor You've given us. Help us learn to fight spiritual battles with spiritual weapons. In Jesus's name, amen!

Day 3
Belt of Truth

Ephesians 6:14a states, "*Stand firm therefore, HAVING GIRDED YOUR LOINS WITH TRUTH.*"
To understand this piece of armor, you must know what or who truth is. Look up John 8:31–32 and fill in the blanks:
"*If you abide in* _____ _____, then *you are truly disciples of Mine; and you shall know the* _____, *and the* _____ *shall make you free.*"
Now look up John 14:6 and do the same:
"*Jesus said to him, 'I am the way, and the* _____, *and the life; no one comes to the Father, but through Me.*'"
Jesus is truth.
If you know Him and His word, you shall be free. But free from what?
You'll be free from believing all the enemy's lies, worrying about what others think, anxiety, and insecurity. You'll be free from fear. Can you believe that?
Sometimes in life, we're faced with circumstances that seem hopeless. We're to stand on truth and believe He'll see us through it. Can you think of anybody in the Bible who trusted God's truth over their circumstances or what they saw right in front of them?

What about Noah? God told him to build a boat, that it was going to rain and flood. Rain, what's rain? It'd never rained before, but Noah believed the truth he knew about God and responded with obedience.
What about Abraham? God promised to make his descendants more numerable than the stars in the sky or the sand on the seashore. He gave him a son through Sarah, like He said He would, then told him to sacrifice that same son of promise. Abraham didn't hesitate for a second! Read Genesis 22:5 and see if you can find the proof. Write it below.

When Abraham is taking Isaac up the mountain, he tells the rest of his young men: *"Stay here with the donkey, and I and the lad will go yonder; and <u>we</u> will worship and return to you."* He had no doubt God would come through with His promises, even if he didn't know how He would do it.

Both men faced earthly sacrifices, and if they stood on God's truth, they'd lose something:

- Noah—he'd lose the respect of those around him; they all thought he was crazy.
- Abraham—he'd lose his son.

How could they be so fearless? They knew the truth and weren't afraid to use it! They cared more about pleasing God than pleasing those around them. Abraham and Noah were looking at their lives from an eternal perspective.

May God teach us to be so bold!

How are you impacting those around you?

Do you stand on His word even if no one stands with you? Or do you compromise to fit in?

If you're not at that point of courage but would like to get closer, read Colossians 3:23 and 1 Thessalonians 2:4. See if you can find some things that will help you stand on God's word and record them below.

In Colossians, Paul talks about relationships, particularly with family. He instructs readers that no matter what they do, they're to do it heartily and for the Lord rather than for men. He goes on, in verse 24, to say we'll receive our eternal reward from the Lord because we serve Him.

What's your motivation? Are you seeking recognition? Justification from your peers or coworkers? To prove yourself worthy?

Paul briefly tells the Thessalonian readers that he's been through some stuff, but he didn't compromise the message because it wasn't his. God entrusted him with the gospel, so he spoke to them *"not as pleasing men but God, who examines our hearts"* (1 Thess. 2:4).

Are you willing to share His word even if it brings persecution? Why or why not?

Paul knew that God's opinion of him was the only one that mattered. Man, I can't wait to get there! I used to dress, act, and speak in ways that would get me noticed by the people around me. I thought their attention was crucial. If I didn't do certain things, I feared they might not want to hang out with me anymore. In my early 20s, I used to go out a bunch, dancing and club-hopping. When the group I hung out with graduated college, we all went our separate ways. That change happened around the same time I got married and started spending time alone with God, and He began to show me who I was in Him.

One of those friends also got married, so we all went to the wedding. These people who I'd partied with for so many years thought things would pick right back up where they left off. And they did for the most part, but when I told them I didn't do that stuff anymore, they couldn't believe it. I still love them as my friends, and we still had a good time together, but how they see me has changed. They don't just see me as entertainment anymore, and guess what…they still love me.

JLT #8—Let's talk about your testimony for a second. Did you know that if people are still inviting you to parties where they'll be doing things you no longer do, there's something wrong with your testimony? If you really have changed, and God is really working in your life, they should know better than to invite you to something like that. Are you still trying to appease those around you, or is God your main focus? Read Luke 6:26. We should speak out about our faith *in love*, *with boldness*, and not worry what people think about it. If everybody's happy with us, we may need to reevaluate things. After all, the Lord calls us to be different.

So, how do you get on the path of change?

By spending time alone with God. What do you think it means to spend time alone with the Father?

Spending time alone with the Lord is kind of like dating. In the beginning, you're both on your best behavior: not taking food off each other's plate, wearing your best clothes around each other, etc. But after the first few dates, you start to let the walls down. Your flaws begin to show, and you begin to trust that person to love you anyway.

God does love you anyway because He knitted you in your mother's womb (Ps. 139:13), and He knows how many hairs are on your head (Luke 12:7). He wants nothing more than for you to run to Him with anything and everything. Did you know that He knows what you're thinking anyway (Ps. 139:2)?

Why *don't* you go to Him?

Why not go to the source of all things for help, advice, and direction?

> **JLT #9**—If you really want to see the depth of God's love for you, read Matthew 6:25–34, where it tells you how much He cares for the birds and the lilies but how much more He loves us and will provide all things. And if you really, *really* want to put it all into perspective, read Job 38–39, where He goes into detail about all the things He created and cares about. All the details and emotions displayed in Job, yet He still loves us more. It's humbling!

So, why is it best to spend some time *alone* with the Lord?

I think you can probably figure that one out…because all the things that surround us on a daily basis are noisy. He speaks in a still, small voice that's impossible to hear unless you quiet down the distractions.

The more you get to know Him, run to Him for all things, and trust Him as your best friend, the more He'll show you how to overcome the enemy. James 4:7 says, *"Submit therefore to God. Resist the devil and he will flee from you."*

I don't think it's a good idea to fully submit to someone you don't know. Let's look at it from a dating perspective since we were just talking about that. You wouldn't give a guy on a first date the information for your bank account, would you? Why not?

Because you don't know him well enough yet to know if he'll take the money and run.

The same concept applies with God but in the opposite way. When we don't know Him well enough to fully trust Him, it prevents Him from revealing things to us, either about ourselves or Himself. But once we give ourselves to Him, He begins to change us from the inside out.

He'll show you how to resist the devil as you seek Him. I know it sounds like a "duh" moment, but I didn't realize that for so long. I assumed that every thought that came into my head was a real and valid point I had to at least consider.

Have you ever thought things like, "I'm not smart enough to understand the Bible" or "How could God love me? I've done X, Y, and Z."

You can make X, Y, and Z whatever you've done in your life that makes you think you're not good enough for the Father's love. Ladies, listen good on this one…*those are lies straight from the pit*. They sound like the truth because they're in your accent or dialect, in your head, but they aren't.

Read Romans 6:6 and see if you can find out what happens when we trust Christ as Lord and Savior.

When we ask God to forgive us of our sins, trust that Jesus died on the cross to save us, and accept Him as Lord and Savior, He takes our sinful nature away. It's gone, eradicated, and crucified on the cross with Him (Rom. 6:6 and Gal. 2:20). The power of sin no longer holds us hostage, and we can stand against it. We can *choose* not to believe the enemy's lies.

So how do you know if something is a truth or a lie?

Do you consider the thoughts that come into your head? Or do you just act on them?

The first thing we should do is take all thoughts to Him in prayer.

Then, run it through sixty-six books (I'm referring to the Protestant Bible). If an idea condemns your person—in other words, if it tells you you're no good—it's a lie.

Write Romans 8:1 below.

After you become a child of God, there's no more condemnation. Yes, the Holy Spirit convicts us of our sin when we do something wrong, but it's not Him saying, "Hey, dummy, you screwed up!" It's more like a parent telling you you've dropped the ball, how to move forward, and how to avoid ending up here again.

That's where the belt of truth comes in. Ephesians 6:14 says, *"having girded,"* which means to surround or enclose around something. We are to surround ourselves with truth.

How do you think you can surround yourself with truth?

Look at the activities below and see if they'll draw you closer to the truth or not. Draw a line to the answer **Yes** or **No**.

Playing video games
Shopping for shoes   **Yes**
Reading the Bible
Hanging out with believers   **No**
Continuously spending time in prayer
Watching Lifetime movies about affairs and scandal

Surrounding yourself with truth will be like being surrounded by a filter, a coffee filter for example. The job of a coffee filter is to prevent the coffee grounds from getting into the cup. The cup is only supposed to have liquid in it. If we consider truth as our filter, it should keep out everything that's not truth. The more truth you surround yourself with, the more riff raff it'll keep out of your life.

I breezed past anxiety and insecurity earlier, but let's take a quick look. How can knowing the truth set you free?

In **JLT #9**, where you read Matthew 6:25–34, it talked about how He provides all your needs if you seek Him and His kingdom first. That statement is *very* freeing, but let's discuss how we get there.

What makes us anxious or insecure?

One of the questions earlier in this section was, "Do you compromise to fit in?" I know it seems redundant, but I'll ask it again, and I want you to really think about it and be honest (it can help you). Do you?

Fitting in is one of the biggest reasons for anxiety and insecurity in our lives. We're so desperate to belong or have others accept us, we'll do things we know we shouldn't.

May the God of heaven reveal this truth to you today! In Jesus's name, amen.

Learning His opinion of me was the only one that mattered was a game changer for me. Ladies, listen up. We desire for people to notice us, to want to hang around us because we're fun and because people enjoy our company. But if we act, talk, and dress like this world so the people around us will want to hang out with us, we've missed the point of life. *We're supposed to be different.*

We are to be light to a dark world. If we're desperately trying to fit in with a dark world, how can we be the light they need? Is being light, and being different than everybody else, worth it? Or would you rather be like everybody else? Think about that for a minute.

Why are fads so popular? Because they're unique. They're something we've not seen before. Do you remember when fidget spinners came out? Everybody and their mama had to have one. Not because they were so much fun but because they were different. That's the point, y'all. Different draws attention to itself. God's not able to draw attention to Himself through us if we look, act, and talk like everybody else.

God, may we come to know Your truth more and more each day. May it be a security blanket to us that we crawl under when the world gets us down. May You be our source of comfort and control. In Jesus's name, amen!

Day 4
Breastplate of Righteousness

E phesians 6:14b states, "*and HAVING PUT ON THE BREASTPLATE OF RIGHTEOUSNESS.*" Righteousness means morally right or justifiable—right with God. Write 2 Corinthians 5:21 below.

Write 1 Peter 2:24 below.

Jesus took on *our* sin so we could take on *His* righteousness. *Mind blown!* And not only that, but because of Christ's sacrifice, we've died to sin so we can live in righteousness. Sin, which used to be as natural as breathing to us, is dead, and righteousness becomes our new instinct.

Let that sink in for a minute. Think about it…could you give up your life for people you know will hate you? If that doesn't prove Christ's love for all mankind, I'm not sure anything could.

And to put the icing on the cake, once you're placed into Christ, the Father sees you as He sees Christ, which is righteous.

Look up the following verses and match them to how God sees you:
1. Hebrews 10:14   a) fellow heir with Christ
2. Colossians 1:22   b) holy, blameless

3. Romans 8:17   c) complete
4. Colossians 2:10   d) saint
5. Romans 1:7, Colossians 1:2   e) perfected, sanctified

Earlier in the study, we talked about how we *were* sinners. That tells us there's been a change (we've trusted Jesus as Lord and Savior) and it happened in the past.

What can you tell me about the past?

It's gone. You can't change it or go back to it. We **were** born sinners, spiritually dead to God. Now, we **are** saints who sometimes sin. No matter how badly we screw things up, God won't be mad at us or love us any less.

Read Romans 8:38–39 and write all the things that can't separate us from Him.

Regardless of what we do, *nothing* can separate us from His love. Isn't that awesome news? Don't get me wrong. There will be consequences while on earth, but nobody can take us out of His hand. You can neither save nor un-save yourself. It's all about Him and what He did and continues to do for us.

Warriors used to wear a breastplate in battle. It was designed to protect your torso from injury since your torso contains many vital organs, your heart being one of the most essential. The physical need to protect your heart and other body parts is obvious, but what about the spiritual? Can you think of a reason you'd need to protect your heart spiritually?

Let's see what the Bible says about it. Look up these verses and write what they say about the heart: Matthew 12:34b, Proverbs 4:23, 1 Samuel 16:7, and Romans 10:10.

The passage in Romans tells us that with the heart a man believes, resulting in righteousness.

We must protect what we allow into our hearts. If our treasure is where our hearts will be, we've got to make sure not to treasure anything more than God. Not popularity, not status, not fame and fortune. Nothing should matter to us as much as He does. Remember, He knows the truth. He can see what's really in your heart, even if you've hidden it from others. If you fill your heart with ungodly things or allow a bunch of junk to get in there, it'll distract you and will eventually take your focus off the Lord. Living your life with the

Almighty as your treasure is how others will see Him in you. If we're focused on other things, they may miss the opportunity to see Him and the chance to know more.

God, I know the enemy hates for people to realize who they are in You. Insecurities melt away. Anxieties become manageable and even start to disappear. Your power changes lives. May You show us who we are to You and how precious we are to You. May we see ourselves as You do. In Jesus's name, amen!

Day 5
Gospel of Peace

Ephesians 6:15 reads, *"having shod YOUR FEET WITH THE PREPARATION OF THE GOSPEL OF PEACE."*

When I taught preschool-aged kids, I called this piece of armor "speedy shoes." The idea was for them to always be ready to move and share. If we were to win the lottery, we'd tell everybody we knew and saw, and we'd probably think about shouting it from the rooftops. The gospel is so much better than winning the lottery because it's eternal, so we should be wanting to shout it from the rooftops even more. But let me ask you a question. Could you give a book report on a book you hadn't read? What about a movie you hadn't seen?

It'd be difficult, right? If you're a smooth talker, you may be able to offer some details, but what you say would be general, vague, and shallow.

The same goes for spreading the gospel. If you don't spend time alone with God to get to know Him intimately, what are you going to say about Him? If you don't know Him very well, your testimony could also be *general, vague, and shallow*. People who are genuinely seeking Him may see through your generalities and move on to somebody who can provide more truth.

Why would you want to tell anybody about the gospel?

Why do you tell people about a really good sale?

Why do you tell everybody at work about a great movie you watched?

Why do you tell your besties about an awesome recipe you made recently?

Because you want them to have the same experience you had, right? Well, how much more fun is heaven going to be than hell? We should be telling everybody we see about Jesus and how they can come to know Him. There's nothing we could ever share that'll have a greater impact on the lives of those around us.

The gospel, once we believe and accept it, brings peace.

Read Romans 5:1 (NASB), and fill in the blanks:

"*Therefore, having been* _____ *by* _____, *we have* _____ *with God through our Lord Jesus Christ.*"

Now from your own mind, see if you can define these words.

Justified—

Faith—

Peace—

Look them up, Google them, whatever you like to do, and see if it adds more depth. Here's what I found:

Justified—made right with God; acquit, clear from any charge or imputation; *free*.

Faith—trust, belief; complete confidence in someone or something.

Peace—freedom from disturbance; tranquility; a state or period in which there is no war, or the war has ended; *rest*; well-being, bliss, quietness.

In other words, once our faith in Jesus makes us right with God and we accept His ability to save us, we can rest in the Father. We can rest in Him while He works and lives His life through us. Whew!

Once you're placed into Christ, the moment you cry out, ask Him to forgive your sins, and trust Him to save you, you have peace with God. Did you hear me? You have peace with God. The Creator of the universe isn't mad at you. He has cast your sin as far as the east is from the west (Ps. 103:12) and remembers them no more (Heb. 8:12). I know I've already used those verses, but they're worth repeating.

He loves all people so much that He sent His only Son (John 3:16) to take away the sin of the world (John 1:29). The truth of the Bible is that it's God's love letter to us. The Father tells us through it that He wants to spend time with us, for us to come to Him with our heavy burdens (Matt. 11:28–29), and to love Him with all our heart, soul, mind, and strength (Mark 12:30).

Let's see what else the Bible says about peace. Match up the following verses to their meaning:

John 16:33   *"The steadfast of mind Thou wilt keep in perfect peace, because he trusts in Thee."*

2 Thessalonians 3:16   *"In Me you may have peace. In the world you have tribulation, but take courage; I have overcome the world."*

Isaiah 26:3   *"Now may the Lord of peace Himself continually grant you peace in every circumstance."*

Did you notice the contrast in John 16:33? He is contrasting being in the world versus being in Him. In the world, we have tribulation. In the Lord, we have peace.

What's the opposite of peace?

I Googled it and found noise, irritation, conflict, or *fear*. The opposite of peace is fear. The enemy knows that too and does his best to keep us in fear.

Do you live in fear? Being honest here can really help you move forward and learn how *not* to be fearful.

What are you afraid of?

Fear sometimes leads to anxiety. What are you anxious about?

Earlier, in the belt of truth, we talked about anxiety and how it causes us to do things we know are wrong so we'll fit in. We also see that anxiety robs us of our peace, which reminds me of my younger days when I was an athlete. I was under significant pressure, mostly from myself but also from my family and coaches. When I was at the height of my career, I got a mental block. I'm not sure if you've had one, but they're real, y'all. I knew I was physically able to do what I was trying to do, but my body just would not cooperate.

I looked ridiculous, I felt ridiculous, and it was the most frustrating thing I'd ever experienced. The more I tried to get over it, the worse the block got. My mom was upset with me. My coaches were upset with me. I was upset with myself. Those months were some of the darkest times of my life. The stress got so bad that the thought of going to the gym made me nauseous. I was anxious every day about having to go to the gym, but if I wasn't there, I was worried about what I'd miss. Eventually, I figured out that my only option was to quit, so I did. Other than being saved, it was the most freeing experience I'd ever had up to that point in my life. I could finally breathe again!

It'd seem from my story that my advice on anxiety is to quit. Since that doesn't sound like the best suggestion, let's see what the Bible says about how to deal with it. Read the following verses and note what you see about how to handle anxiety: Psalm 94:17–23, Philippians 4:6–7, and 1 Peter 5:7.

The verses from the book of Psalms tell us that when anxious thoughts overwhelm us, it's His comforting thoughts that delight our soul (Ps. 94:19). Philippians tells us not to be anxious but in everything let our requests be known to God (Phil. 4:6). Is that all it says, though?

Keep reading.

We need to also notice that the passages instruct us to bring everything to God by prayer and supplication (crying out in desperation and humility) with thanksgiving. We don't just make a "grocery list" of things we need or want. We should cry out to Him in humility and reverence. When we do, His peace will wash over us and *guard our hearts* and minds in Christ Jesus (Phil. 4:7). Praying in humility and reverence will help us pray within His will and show us when we're not.

In other words, Jesus is the only true cure for anxiety. Sure, there are other things like self-help books, therapists, or even pills that can help the issue for a while. But when you finish the book, complete your sessions, or run out of the prescription, the issue is still there. The methods listed above do help and can be productive in creating real change, but God is the only one who can *remove* the struggle or give you the grace to walk through it.

JLT #10—If you read Romans 1:7, 1 Corinthians 1:3, 2 Corinthians 1:2, Galatians 1:3, Ephesians 1:2, Philippians 1:2, and Colossians 1:2, you'll see that Paul begins all his letters with the greeting: *"Grace to you and peace from God our Father."* It'd seem to me that since grace always precedes peace, you'd need to first have grace before you can truly enjoy peace. Most people define "grace" as unmerited favor, which is true, but I've also heard it defined as the desire and power to do God's will. In 2 Corinthians 12:7–10, Paul talks about his thorn in the flesh. The verses don't say exactly what the thorn was, but he wanted it gone! He asked God three times to remove it (12:8), but God didn't. He told Paul (paraphrasing), "My grace is sufficient. My power is perfected in your weakness" (12:9). Until we realize that any good deed we do is because of His life in us, we probably won't truly have or enjoy peace. Remember how we defined peace before, as rest, tranquility, or the absence of war. If we're striving to do things in our own strength, we are neither at rest nor allowing Him to be our strength.

I wish I could tell you to do A, B, and C and the anxiety and insecurity would vanish, but it's a process. Here are some things I do that have led me in the right direction:

- Prayer
- Spending time in the Word
- Taking care what I watch and listen to and who I hang out with

Good in = good out
Bad in = bad out

God, today's topic is complex. The enemy will hit us hard if we pray to You about anxiety and insecurity because a prayer like that is the key to his undoing. If we start to understand that we don't have to live in fear anymore, he loses his grip on us. He can't keep us cowering in the corner anymore. May You teach us as we seek You to let Your peace outweigh the fear. In Jesus's name, amen!

WEEK 4
Day 1
Gospel of Peace (Continued)

We ended last week with *good in = good out, bad in = bad out*.

It sounds like something your mom would say, doesn't it? I know…but it's true. I have a past I'm not proud of, but I'm learning to see it as a blessing. Because of my experiences, I can reach others going down a similar path and hopefully spare them years of pain and consequences. It does make for a slippery slope, though. I really have to watch who I hang out with and where we go. There are certain things or places that take me back so quickly I don't even realize it. Just listening to a song from that time of my life puts me in that frame of mind again. It's scary how fast I'm tempted to revert back to that lifestyle if I'm not paying attention. Jackie used to say, "We learn with difficulty and forget with ease." And how right he was.

Did you know that one of the reasons the Dead Sea is "dead" is because there are no outlet streams? All the minerals flow in with nowhere to go. The concentration is so dense that no wildlife or vegetation can survive. The things God reveals to us aren't supposed to stay with us either. Once we realize how great God is and receive His peace, we're supposed to share it with others. That's where the "speedy shoes" come in.

Have you ever been given the opportunity to share how He's changed your life with somebody but didn't? Why or why not?

It can be intimidating to share, especially when the enemy says, "You can't tell them anything. What if they ask you for the chapter and verse? You don't know that." I experienced that situation while writing this book. I went to a Bible study on Wednesday mornings, and a story about my past popped into my head.

Back in the day, I had a friend I hung out with all the time. She also had another girl she hung out with besides me. Her other friend and I didn't see eye to eye on some things because I was a bad influence on our friend, and she was a good influence. I constantly gave her buddy a hard time. She handled it like a champ, though, never talking bad about us but encouraging us both to do the right thing. She suffered righteously (which was what the lesson was on that day) because of me. I can see how I've been blessed because of her obedience.

I felt the Holy Spirit calling me to share that story. So, I did by emailing it to the teacher. I told her I was emailing it because if I tried to share in class, I'd just cry the whole time (and I so would). My assumption was that sending the teacher a message would be good enough…but not so much.

See, I had been praying for weeks prior to that for God to use me as He saw fit, that I wanted to be His go-to girl. "Here I am, Lord. Send me" (Isa. 6:8 paraphrased). He answered my prayers by asking me to share, and I gave Him the feeble effort of emailing my teacher. I did what He asked, right? Well, my teacher responded by saying I had a great testimony and that she hoped I'd strongly consider sharing in class. *Busted*. When I read that, I heard the Holy Spirit telling me He needed more.

There I was, praying all this time for Him to use me as He saw fit, but the first time He called me to move, the first time *He* answered *my* prayer, I said, "Ohhhh yeah, I don't like to share in class because it makes me cry, so what else you got?" That hit me like a ton of bricks!

The enemy knows insecurity and fear will cause us not to do things God asks of us. Why do you think he plays them up so much? Satan will do everything in his power to exaggerate, highlight, and remind us of our fear and anxiety because if we're focused on fear and anxiety, we're not focused on God.

So, I spent the entire next week in prayer about it. "Okay, I hear You! I know You're calling me to share. I'm terrified. I always cry when I talk about You or anything You've done in my life because it means so much to me, but I'm going to step out in faith and share regardless of what happens." That was my actual prayer, y'all. Once I made up my mind that I was sharing, I was hit with, "What if they start to think I'm one of those girls who cries all the time so when I start to share, they all roll their eyes and tune me out?" That is a lie straight from the pit! If I cried the whole time, who cares? If I sounded like a country hick, so what? If nobody understood a word that came out of my mouth, no worries. *The only opinion of me I needed to worry about was His.* I kept telling myself that time and time again over that next week. I committed, in prayer, that I was going to share no matter what, and I did. It was quick, to the point, and guess what? I didn't cry.

I'd been praying that He'd use me as His go-to girl, but for Him to do that, He had to know that I'd do whatever He called me to do, no matter how it made me feel, who would be in the audience, or what the outcome would be. The results weren't up to me anyway (that's His thing).

If you do decide to step out in faith and share the gospel, what will you say?

The most common way to talk to unbelievers about coming to salvation in Jesus is the Romans Road.

- *"For all have sinned and fall short of the glory of God"* (Rom. 3:23).
- *"For the wages of sin is death, but the free gift of God is eternal life in Christ Jesus our Lord"* (Rom. 6:23).
- *"But God demonstrates His own love toward us, in that while we were yet sinners, Christ died for us"* (Rom. 5:8).
- *"That if you confess with your mouth Jesus as Lord, and believe in your heart that God raised Him from the dead, you shall be saved; for with the heart man believes, resulting in righteousness, and with the mouth he confesses, resulting in salvation"* (Rom. 10:9–10).
- *"For WHOEVER WILL CALL UPON THE NAME OF THE LORD WILL BE SAVED"* (Rom. 10:13).

I hope that's old news to you, but it's crucial we all know there's more to salvation than walking somebody through these verses or repeating a prayer someone else tells you to pray. It's a personal relationship with Jesus Christ.

You must first realize you need a Savior. The fact that you need more than just you in a world that's constantly telling you that you don't is hard to grasp. Admitting you're wrong, asking for help, and submitting to Jesus to be Lord of your life isn't something the world is used to doing.

The Romans Road isn't the only way to share, either. It can be as simple as telling somebody how He's changed your life. You don't have to be a Bible scholar to talk to people about God. Look at the man born blind who Jesus healed in John 9. The Pharisees were upset because Jesus healed him on the Sabbath, so they questioned the man. He told them what Jesus did and that he thought Jesus was a prophet (9:13–17). They didn't believe him, so they questioned his parents. They didn't provide the answers they were looking for and told the Pharisees if they wanted to know, to ask their son (9:18–21). So, they did, again. He finally said, *"Whether He is a sinner, I do not know; one thing I do know, that, whereas I was blind, now I see"* (9:25).

Not much is known about the man except that he used to sit and beg (9:8). Since he was blind from birth, and school wasn't as common as it is today, I'm guessing he lacked education. But Jesus took away his blindness and gave him sight, so he wasn't afraid to share. He told them all he knew; that he was blind but now he could see. Telling your story can be that simple.

Remember, when sharing with others, the results aren't up to you. God's in charge of that. Just like being intimidated to share, we can also get frustrated or jaded that we *are* sharing but nobody is listening. *"So then neither the one who plants nor the one who waters is anything, but God who causes the growth"* (1 Cor. 3:7).

God, speaking of fear, sometimes we're afraid to share You with others. What will they think if I speak of my faith? Will they still want to hang out with me? These are questions that come to mind, but really, our only question must be, "What will You think?" Your opinion of me is the only one that matters. May You teach us that as we seek You. In Jesus's name, amen!

Day 2
Shield of Faith

Ephesians 6:16 reads, *"In addition to all, taking up the shield of faith with which you will be able to extinguish all the flaming missiles of the evil one."*

Notice verse 16 starts with "in addition to all, taking up." For the first three pieces of armor, Paul uses the word "having" before the action he describes. For example, having girded (belt of truth), having put on (breastplate of righteousness), and having shod (gospel of peace, "speedy shoes"). Paul's word choice tells us that people should wear the first three pieces of armor at all times. The next three are meant to be "taken up" as needed.

So far, we've surrounded ourselves with truth, protected our hearts by knowing that we're right with God, and have the peace that passes understanding by accepting the free gift of the Lord's salvation.

Can you think of any reason why we need to take up faith on top of all that?

First, it's a bit like building blocks. It's difficult to have faith without truth, knowing truth allows you to see that you're righteous in Him, and knowing who you are in Him brings peace.

Second, I believe Paul knew that when something good happens for God, the enemy shows up. And he doesn't just show up—he shows up bigger and badder than ever before. Satan despises when you mature spiritually because that means his power over you diminishes. The enemy has less control over your life and understands that the more you know about God, the more impact you'll have on others for His kingdom. Have you ever noticed that the enemy doesn't really attack those openly sinning? They're doing enough damage on their own, so the devil doesn't have to waste his time on them.

When you start to mature spiritually and put on the first three pieces of armor, your faith will begin to protect you from the devil's tricks, including his lies about who you are (and whose you are) and the temptation of doubt.

Write out Hebrews 11:1, and underline what it says about faith.

Definition of faith—complete *trust* or *confidence* in something or someone; having no doubt; confident expectation.

Some say faith is like the wind. You can't see it, but you can see where it's been and the effect it has on the things it touches (consider tornado and/or hurricane damage). When you pull out a chair, you're confident it'll hold you, so you sit down without hesitation. Upon walking across a suspension bridge hanging over a deep gorge, you're a little more cautious, right?

How is your faith in Christ as your Lord and Savior? Like the chair? Or like the bridge?

If you're still like the bridge, hang in there.

How do we get more faith? Romans 10:17 says, *"So faith comes from hearing, and hearing by the word of Christ."* Faith comes by hearing, but hearing what? Hearing your favorite song on the radio? No. "Hearing" can happen by listening to others preach the good news of the gospel. We can also hear by listening to the voice of the Holy Spirit.

Look up the following verses and match them to what the Spirit does for us:

John 14:26	instructs us
Nehemiah 9:20	speaks through us in tough times
Mark 13:11	teaches us all things and helps us remember

Think of it this way…the more you do something, the more comfortable you become. For example, the first time you skydive, you're probably going to be terrified. You know the guy *says* the parachute will open and prevent you from plummeting to your death, but you've not actually experienced that happening yet. In your *mind*, you're 100 percent sure (because he said it's true and you believe him), but your *body* isn't there yet. Your body is doubting the decision big time.

You're shaking like a leaf, your palms are sweaty, your heart is racing, and your stomach is in knots. But you go through with it, and you see that what he said *was* true. You do it again, and again, and again, and before you know it, your body is catching up with your mind. You don't feel sick anymore, your hands are only a little sweaty, and your heart is racing from excitement instead of fear.

When the Father first saves you, your faith is so new and intellectual (meaning it's mostly in your head) that you still have doubts and questions. As you sit at God's feet and in His word, listening to Him teach you, you'll start to understand more. Once you seek

Him, He'll start to reveal things to you in a way only He can. The Lord, through the Holy Spirit, takes the information in your head and moves it into your heart, making it revelation. The more revelation you have from the Lord, the less doubt and questions you have. Less doubt and questions equal more faith because you start believing that what God says is really true! Therefore, the more you abide with the Creator—letting Him transform the information into revelation, *hearing* Him teach you directly from His heart to yours—the more faith you'll have.

I feel like we need to camp out with Nehemiah's verse for a minute. God does use tribulation, or tough times, to mature us spiritually and grow our faith. Have you ever heard people say, "You won't know how bad you need God until He's all you have"? It's so true, y'all.

Read Romans 5:3–5 and James 1:2–4 and see if you can recognize the progression. Write it below.

Exult in tribulation, tribulation brings perseverance, perseverance brings proven character, proven character brings hope, and hope doesn't disappoint (paraphrase of the Romans verses).

Consider it all joy, knowing that the testing of your faith produces endurance (steadfastness), and endurance's perfect result ends with you being perfect (spiritually mature), lacking nothing (paraphrase of the James verses).

There are many passages in the Bible where the writers tell the reader that being a Christ follower will be difficult. One example is from Jesus, and He puts it this way: "*If the world hates you, you know that it has hated Me before it hated you. If you were of the world, the world would love its own; but because you are not of the world, but I chose you out of the world, therefore the world hates you*" (John 15:18–19).

Faith is a vital part of life on earth. Down here, on the enemy's course, we've got to have faith that God is who He says He is and that He did a perfect work through Jesus. Because of all that, we know the end of the story, which is eternal life with Him in glory.

If we know the end of the story, we can do what 1 Peter 5:8–10 says. Read those verses, and note what it tells you about the following:

1. Who's after us

2. How we're to fight

3. Why

Satan, our adversary, is who's after us. We must resist him, firm in our faith. We should do all that because after a little while, God will perfect, confirm, strengthen, and establish us.

Above, it says that the end of the story is us spending eternity with Him in glory. But let's be a little more specific. Read 1 Thessalonians 4:16–17.

- The dead in Christ shall rise first.
- All who are alive and remain shall be caught up together with them in the clouds to meet the Lord in the air.
- We shall always be with God.

Now read 1 Peter 1:3–9 and note what it says about faith.

According to these verses, we are…

- Born again to a living hope (1:3).
- To obtain an imperishable inheritance reserved in heaven (1:4).
- Protected by the power of God through *faith* for a salvation that's to be revealed in the last time (1:5).
- Rejoicing in salvation, though for now we have trials (1:6).
- Aware that the proof (genuineness) of our *faith* may result in praise, glory, and honor at the resurrection of Jesus Christ (1:7)
- Obtaining the outcome of our *faith*, the salvation of our soul (1:9).

Isn't that enough to keep us from living a defeated life?

No matter what happens to us, we'll end up with Jesus! That's our shield of faith right there.

The world says, "I'll believe it when I see it." Believers say, "I'll see it when I believe it." Look up one more passage, then we'll move on. Find 2 Kings 6:8–20. What stands out to you in these verses?

What a powerful story. The king of Aram was planning to attack Israel. The Israelites discovered the plot because Elisha gave warning. The king was upset about it and told his men to go get Elisha. They went down to Dothan to seize him. When they arrived, Elisha's servant said, "*Alas, my master! What shall we do?*" (6:15). Elisha said not to worry about it because "*those who are with us are more than those who are with them*" (6:16).

Can you imagine? Being surrounded by all those horses and soldiers who are trying to capture you when you're just two people.

Or so you thought.

Elisha's servant was probably freaking out a little bit. I know I would be. Unless I saw what Elisha saw. He prayed that the Lord would open his servant's eyes. He did, and the man now saw what Elisha did. There was a full company of horses and chariots of fire on the mountain all around them.

Y'all, the Father is fighting for you even if you don't see it. The more faith we have, the more of Him we'll see.

God, I come to You today to beg and plead for these ladies. I know the difference that knowing You has made in my life, and I want that for them as well. May You meet them in their studies and show them how to make time for You in their busy lives and seek You. Not to know more about the Bible, or to quote scripture to others, but to have a more intimate relationship with You. God, may You pour out Your blessing as they depend on You more and more each day. In Jesus's name, amen!

Day 3
Helmet of Salvation

Ephesians 6:17 states, *"And take THE HELMET OF SALVATION."*
Knowing you're saved protects your mind and helps you renounce the enemy. We touched on saying no to the devil when we talked about the lust of the flesh, but we're going to dive a little deeper here.

Have you ever seen *Labyrinth* with David Bowie and Jennifer Connelly?

Spoiler Alert

The main character, Sarah, wants to go out, but her parents make her stay home and babysit her baby brother. She's upset about it and wishes her brother would disappear. While she's reading a book, she falls asleep, becomes one of the main characters in the book, and the goblin king (David Bowie's character) kidnaps her brother. On her adventure to find her brother, Sarah fights through many trials and mazes and has to face a bunch of goofy villains. When she finally gets to the palace, where her brother is, she figures out the goblin king's game. Sarah says to him, "You have no power over me!" When she speaks those words, everything falls apart, melts away, and she's back home with her brother in his room where she left him.

I know it's a silly illustration, but it shows how powerful knowing the end of the story is. Like we discussed with the shield of faith, we'll end up eternally in heaven. We know the end of the story and understand that once the Father redeems us, our adversary has no power over us.

This concept is a big one, y'all.

Write out James 4:7 below.

Why do you think it's essential to protect your head (other than to keep your brain inside)?

Remember back when we talked about the breastplate of righteousness and protecting your heart? How does bad stuff get into your heart?

It goes through your mind. The good news is that you have the authority to allow it to enter or not. But how?

Let's see what the Bible says about it. Look up these verses and see if you can spot the progression:

- Romans 12:1–2
- Colossians 3:2
- 2 Corinthians 10:3–5
- 1 Corinthians 2:16

Paul starts by telling his readers not to be conformed to the world but to be transformed by the renewing of their minds.

But how?

By setting their mind on things above and not the things that are on the earth.

But how?

By taking every thought captive to destroy speculations and every lofty thing raised up against the knowledge of God.

But how?

Because we *have the mind of Christ*. We can yield to His life in us, or defer to His way of thinking, and respond as He would.

If you go back a little in Ephesians, Paul tells the readers to no longer walk as the Gentiles (lost people) do, in the futility of their minds. The Greek word for futility is *mataiotes* and is described as transientness, depravity, vanity, and emptiness. It also connects to the Hebrew word for folly, perverseness, and wickedness. The point of the story is that we have a new mind, the mind of Christ, so we don't have to accept the enemy's lies anymore!

In 1 Peter 1:13, readers see they should gird their minds for action, fixed on the hope of grace that Christ will reveal when he returns. Remember from learning about the belt of truth, "to gird" means "to surround." You're to surround your mind with the hope (confident expectation) of your salvation. Knowing and dwelling on the fact that the Father has saved you will help you remember that the enemy has no power over you.

True or False: Every thought that pops into your head is from God.

You should know the answer already because we've covered it. But, since we're talking about protecting what we allow into our minds, I thought it was relevant to repeat.

False! The enemy uses your mind and often prevails because the world's system has told us that if it feels right, it must be okay. Well, guess what…it's not. Emotions, thoughts, and feelings lie, y'all. They run through our brain, which is in our flesh, and guess who has access to it? Yep, the enemy, but he can only do what we allow him to do.

That's why it's essential to know verses like 2 Corinthians 10:3–5. We're stopping every thought that comes into our heads, and we're putting it through an imaginary customs check, like in the airport. We stop it when it first arrives and analyze it through the X-ray machines (through sixty-six books), and if everything is safe, it can go through. If not, you should discard the thought and ignore it.

True or False: Being tempted to _____ (fill in the blank) is just as bad as doing it. False.

Read Hebrews 4:15 and note below what it says about Jesus's temptation.

He was tempted in all things as we are, yet without sin. If it *is* just as sinful for us to be tempted, then how could Jesus be without sin? Let's keep reading. Look up James 1:12–18 (focusing on verse 15). Write what stands out to you about our mind and temptation.

The enemy uses our minds to introduce temptation through our own desires and lusts. He doesn't tempt me to binge-watch baseball because that's not something I normally gravitate to. He tempts me with eating a whole box of Swiss cake rolls. Once Satan presents the temptation, you have the choice to act on it or not. When you choose to act on it, your desire has conceived. When your desire conceives, it gives birth to sin. It's a process.

The enemy doesn't want you to know that!

That's why he distracts you with things of the world. When your mind is distracted, your thoughts, emotions, and feelings will be allowed to sneak past customs so that anything and everything gets through.

The good news is that you can stop the process of sin. The X-ray machine of your imaginary customs station is the Bible's sixty-six books.

What do you think it means to run something through sixty-six books?

It means to take it through the whole thing. If a thought or option doesn't line up with all of the Bible, you should avoid it. If it aligns with Facebook, Instagram, TikTok, or Snapchat…beware. If what you're tempted to do lines up with the world, run in the opposite direction. After all, we are to flee from sin and pursue righteousness (2 Tim. 2:22, 1 Cor. 6:18, and 1 Tim. 6:11).

One more thing about fleeing from sin. I've heard young people ask the following question about dating: "How far can I go before it becomes sin?" That's a fair question. I know our emotions get a little crazy when we're young, but we must run from sin! You should never try to see how close you can get to sin without actually sinning. That's a slippery slope few can survive without consequences.

Flee young people, flee.

The good news…write 1 Corinthians 10:13 below to find out.

He won't give us more than we can handle, and He always provides a way out. *Whew, thank You, Lord!*

God, may You reveal to us our forgiven state in which You allow us to continuously live. No more asking for forgiveness and no more worrying if we'll still get to go to heaven even though we failed, again. As we live life on earth, may we see life through Your eyes. In Jesus's name, amen.

Day 4
Sword of the Spirit

Ephesians 6:17 reads, *"and the sword of the Spirit, which is the word of God."* Let's review the armor of God really quick.

<u>**Defense**—fighting against attacks</u>
Belt of Truth
Breastplate of Righteousness
Gospel of Peace ("speedy shoes")
Shield of Faith
Helmet of Salvation

<u>**Offense**—the act of attacking</u>
Sword of the Spirit

Notice that the sword of the Spirit is the only offensive weapon we have. The sword of the Spirit is God's word. There are two Greek terms for "word," *logos* and *rhēma*. Here are my simple definitions for them (keep in mind, this is an abbreviated list):

- logos is information
- rhēma is revelation

The one used in verse 17 is, you guessed it, rhēma. God's word will remain in your head (as information) until He, through the Holy Spirit, reveals its true meaning to you, turning it into revelation and writing it on your heart.

God's word is powerful. Can you think of some places in the Bible where God spoke and things happened?

Look up the following and write beside them what happened when God spoke:

Genesis 1:3—

John 4:46–54—

John 11:43–45—

JLT #11—Have you ever wondered why He said, *"Lazarus, come forth"* (John 11:43) instead of just saying, "Come forth"? Maybe because if Christ hadn't specified, He would've resurrected far more people.

God spoke light into existence. He told a man his son was alive, even though the boy was in a different city. He just spoke it, and it was so. He called out to a dead man, told him to come out of the grave, and *he did.*

So, let's see how we can use this power to our advantage. Read Luke 4:1–13. I know it's a lot but bear with me. It'll be worth it. See if you can come up with a plan of attack and write it below.

Right after Jesus was baptized, He was taken into the wilderness for the devil to tempt Him. He was there for forty days and nights and ate nothing during that time. Satan knew that Jesus, in His humanity, would be hungry, so he said, *"If you are the Son of God, tell this stone to become bread"* (Luke 4:3). Jesus's response was, *"It is written"* (4:4). Then He quoted scripture. Satan tempted Him twice more, and both times He referenced scripture. After the third time, the devil fled from Christ.

My pastor says, "You must get into the word until the word gets into you." Once you're seeking God to know Him, He'll start revealing things to you. Once the Father takes the information and makes it revelation, you can then use it to fight the enemy and make him flee. The power of scripture is why your Sunday school teacher worked tirelessly to get you to memorize it. The more you've memorized, the greater your ability to attack. Don't be discouraged if you only know one verse, though. It only takes one...and remember, God is known for doing *a lot* with a little.

JLT #12—A tip for memorizing scripture is to write it with your opposite hand. I know it sounds weird, but it totally works! You have to concentrate so hard on writing that the verse sticks in your mind better.

Since the Bible is our only weapon, we must know how to use it properly. I tell people at work all the time, but we've got to use our words (and, sadly, I'm not a schoolteacher).

Think of ways you can use God's word and write them below.

Let's see what the Bible says about it. Look up the following verses, and record insights you find about God's word.

Hebrews 4:12—

Psalm 119:105—

2 Timothy 3:16—

Isaiah 40:8—

As we close for today, I'd like to discuss memory verses one more time. I know, I know, memorization is hard, time-consuming, and not much fun. *But scripture is our only offensive weapon*, so we've got to keep it with us at all times. It's much easier to combat an attack from the enemy when you can quickly recall a verse from memory instead of saying, "I can't remember; let me Google it really quick."

And let me tell you what else memory verses can be. My husband and I visited a church a few years back, and the pastor talked about memorizing a whole chapter. I thought, "Are you crazy!" But the more he talked about it, the more I wanted to try. So, I did. It took me several weeks, but I got it done.

I said it out loud. I wrote it down. I read, read, and reread it. I spent about fifteen minutes per day going over it. That was four or five years ago, but those verses have become my security blanket. When I have bad dreams, which I often do, instead of lying there replaying the dream over and over in my mind, I start to recite Esther 4. I say it on repeat until the Lord relaxes my mind back to sleep. To me, this is the equivalent of Mom kissing my boo

boo to make it better when I was young. I'm mentally crawling into *His* lap and sitting there until *He* makes it all better. Relying on the word is how we choose not to allow the enemy to control our minds.

Just like everything else, learning the Bible is a process. You've got to memorize His word before you can use it. The process isn't easy either because in the heat of the moment, the devil will do everything in his power to get you to focus on whatever is keeping you up at night (work, money, marriage, etc.). We must train ourselves to go to the scriptures, then to stay there and meditate on Him.

I have a chapter I used to teach kids to memorize. I like it because it's jam packed full of life lessons for all ages. Read Psalm 1.

Verse 1 tells us we'll be blessed if we *don't*:

- Walk in the council of the wicked.
- Stand in the path of sinners.
- Sit in the seat of scoffers.

The progression of walk—stand—sit is interesting.

When you're *walking*, you're following the crowd, moving in the same direction but not sure where you'll stop since you're still weighing your options.

When you *stand*, you're getting comfortable, you've stopped moving, you're considering staying there, but you haven't completely made up your mind.

When you *sit*, you've settled in and made your decision.

Complacency is the way the enemy gets us focused on his lies. Think of it like when you go to the food court in the mall. You're walking through, checking out the restaurants, but haven't decided on anything yet. You're standing next to this one and that one, taking samples to see what's tasting good to you. Then, when you make your decision, you get your food and sit down to eat.

Verse 2 tells us we'll be blessed if we *do*:

- Delight in the law of the Lord.
- Meditate on His law day and night.

Verse 3 tells us how the Father will bless us if we do the stuff in verse 2:

- You'll be like a tree firmly planted by streams of water (never thirsty).
- You'll yield fruit in your season (never hungry).
- Your leaf won't wither (won't run out).
- You'll prosper in whatever you do (victorious).

Verses 4–6 distinguish between those who do what the psalm says and those who choose to ignore it.

If you feel like memorizing a chapter, whether it's this one or not, go for it. You won't be disappointed.

Here's my official scripture memorizing process:

I write out the verse three times: in my normal handwriting, in all caps, and with my left hand. As discussed in JLT #12, writing it with your nondominant hand makes you concentrate on it more than normal.

Finally, I try to say it out loud without looking. If I'm successful and think I'll remember it tomorrow, I write it in a journal, then I'm done. The next day, I first say the verse I learned the day before, and if I remember it, I move on to the next one. I repeat the process with the following verse. I finish with writing all verses in a journal by memory each day. By the time you're up to about ten verses, the first nine are good to go because you've said them and written them consistently over the last ten days or so. The more verses you add, the better you get.

God, may Your word become real to us. May it comfort us when we remember it. May we speak it with boldness in love to our brothers and sisters in Christ and encourage them to walk in Your ways. In Jesus's name, amen!

Day 5
Summary and Closing

Great job! We're on the home stretch.

We've spent this whole study talking about the "course of this world," or the bad course. The final piece of the puzzle is the good course. This final day is where you see how to live in a way that's pleasing to God. Read Proverbs 2.

In verses 1–4, there are some "if" statements. Based on those, what should we be doing? Record your answer below.

It says to "*receive my sayings, and treasure my commandments*" (verse 1), "*make our ear attentive to wisdom, incline our hearts to understanding*" (verse 2), "*cry for discernment, lift your voice for understanding*" (verse 3), and see wisdom as treasure and search for it (verse 4 paraphrased).

Let's unpack that a little bit.

The verbs (action words) in these four verses are intrinsically motivated. They imply that the person doing those things is doing it for themselves, not to win a prize, get noticed, or receive a promotion. Their own personal growth is the motivational factor. That's crucial when you're in pursuit of God. To seek Him for any other reason than to know His heart will only limit your reach.

JLT #13—Did you know it's possible not to accept the Bible as truth? What a scary place to be. Jesus talked about it when he said, "*Therefore I speak to them in parables; because while seeing they do not see, and while hearing they do not hear, nor do they understand*" (Matt. 13:13). Many schools of thought today teach you to "know your own truth." If that's you, sister, I'm going to love you enough to tell you that thought process will lead you to an unfulfilling and empty life. You'll be on the throne of your heart and will end up on a roller coaster ride of seeking worldly comfort that'll drive you crazy. And just because *you* don't accept the scriptures as truth doesn't mean they're false. For example, believing that 2+2=6 doesn't change the fact that the answer is four.

When there's an "if" statement, a "then" most likely follows it. That's true in this case as well. Read Proverbs 2:5–9 and write below what will happen if we do the things listed above.

The word "discern" is used several times in Proverbs 2. Look up the definition and record below what you find.

Discern comes from the Hebrew word *bin* and means *to separate mentally*, to perceive, to observe, to pay attention, to be intelligent, to perceive or recognize, and *to distinguish with difficulty* by sight or with other senses.[5]

In the context of the Bible, discernment is being able to see right from wrong according to God's word. Basically, you can separate your own opinion from the truth. You can read a verse, recognize that your opinion of the text has your preconceived notions attached, and ask God to reveal its true meaning to you. With discernment, you can take your thoughts, or what others have taught you, out of the meaning. "What's the text say?" as opposed to "What do I think?" or "What I've heard."

When dealing with people, it can mean to see through pretenses and look straight to the heart of the issue. There was a British show in the '90s called *Keeping Up Appearances*, and it was about a couple doing just that. They weren't super happy with their lives, but only they knew that (or so they hoped) because they made it appear like everything was sunshine and rainbows. Discernment will help us see through the walls people put up. It can help us consider our own walls too.

Verses 6–8 tell us how we get the blessing listed in verses 5 and 9. Read 6–8 and see what I mean. Record what you see below.

---

[5] Strong's Concordance, s.v., "bin," accessed April 18, 2022, https://biblehub.com/hebrew/995.htm

We obtain all those wonderful things because He gives them to us once we seek Him. When you seek the Lord and walk in His ways, God will grant you understanding, protect you, and guide your path. Then, *"wisdom will enter your heart, and knowledge will be pleasant to your soul"* (verse 10), and *"discretion will guard you, understanding will watch over you"* (verse 11).

But why does the Lord do all that? For our protection, but from what? Keep reading (here comes the course of the world again) verses 12–19. What stands out to you in these lines?

Just a side note, verse 13 is a scary one. We can be tempted to fall back into the ways of the world.

One more thing before we move on. When sex and immorality are involved, we tend to think of the man being the bad guy and the woman being the oppressed. Look at verses 16–19. Those lines discuss the "strange woman" who's a smooth talker, abandons what she should be doing or how she should behave, and leads others to death with her ways.

Y'all, being women, we've got to take Proverbs 2 to heart and make sure we're being honest. Have you ever used your femininity to get something? Have you ever flirted with somebody to get a free meal, to get out of a speeding ticket, or to go ahead of a person in line? Men are wired differently than we are. They think about sex more often than we do and are sometimes blinded by it. Knowing we can manipulate men with words and actions can give us an advantage if we're willing to play that card. Don't do it! Just like wearing revealing clothing will attract attention you don't *really* want, so will manipulation. It's a slippery slope that you don't want to approach.

Keep reading, again. Consider what happens if we heed God's words (verses 20–21) and what happens if we don't (verse 22). Write what stands out to you below.

Verses 20–22 spell out the good course and the bad one. When we seek God, He'll protect us from the way of evil (pride), from the perverse man (lust of the eyes: envy, jealousy, cutting corners to get ahead), and the strange woman (lust of the flesh).

One more thing, and we're done. I'm not sure if I've made this clear or not, so here's one last shot. The process of getting off the course of the world and onto His good course isn't easy. Let me ask you a question.

Are you willing to give it all up for Him?

You've got your life going, your kids are great, you have nice things, you get a mani-pedi every other week, you have your favorite TV shows recorded, and your child plays baseball and is a shoo-in for the Little League World Series in the upcoming season. You've got it all.

Would you be willing to give that up to follow Christ? Matthew 16:24–28 talks about walking away from success and material comfort. If you want to save your life, you'll lose it, and if you lose your life for His sake, you'll find it.

Are you willing to lose the life you've built for yourself?

All the fame, fortune, status, and street cred at the ballpark. Are you willing to let it all go to focus on Him and His kingdom? *Do you love Me more than these?*" (John 21:15).

Don't hear what I'm not saying. You can have all that stuff *and* be seeking His kingdom. But sometimes, like with my life, the more I started to seek Him, the more He started changing what I wanted. I used to be the life of the party. I was outspoken, forward, and didn't really care how my actions impacted those around me. I loved shopping and shoes. I've never counted all my pairs of shoes because I'm sure I'd be ashamed of how many there are.

But once I started making Him a priority I wouldn't push to the back burner, He started transforming me into His image. My desires are becoming what He wants. My behaviors are starting to look like how the Lord would act. I don't spend all my money on clothes and shoes anymore. Some of the things I used to love doing (going to fashion week and buying outfits for it only to wear them one time) make me sad now. He has shown me what I missed out on while doing those other things, and I never want to go back there.

God, thank You for our time together in this study. May You walk with us as we go on with our lives and continue to teach us Your ways. May we keep seeking You just to know You. May we let You live Your life through us while we rest. In Jesus's name, amen.

Leader Guide: How to Use This Study to Bring About Meaningful Discussion.

L adies, you've been called to lead this study for a reason; you know there are no coincidences with God. There are probably too many questions for you to discuss them all, and that's good because I want the discussion to be genuine and create real change. I'd love for you to pick the ones that mean something to you. Use your life experiences to bring about deep conversation in your group. If you're not feeling one, don't use it. In fact, you don't have to use any of them if you don't want to. These questions are just a starting point.

I pray for God to use you as He sees fit, for His purpose and for His glory. I pray that you will be blessed in your preparation and that you and your group of ladies finish the study differently than when you all started. I pray that you all have a deeper desire to know God and will continually pursue Him going forward.

Week 1
Did anything stand out to you that you'd like to discuss? Was there any new information?

Leader questions:
Day 1
What does "what you do is not who you are" mean to you?

I grew up watching my dad get mad at something and cuss about it. So, when I got mad growing up, guess what I did…I cussed about it. The more I did that, the more natural that reaction became. Does that mean that's who I am? David was an adulterous murderer (2 Sam. 11–12). Noah got drunk (Gen. 9:20–21). Moses was angry (Exod. 32:19–20). But in the "hall of faith" in Hebrews 11, is any of that bad stuff mentioned? *No.*

We'll discuss who and whose you are later in the course, but for now, start considering that once you've trusted Jesus as Lord and Savior, you're a forgiven child of God, a saint who sometimes sins.

Couple things from Ezekiel 28:

True or False: God's opposite is Satan.

False. God created Satan just like everything else. God has no equal or opposite.

Define wisdom:

Oxford—having experience, knowledge, good judgment, the quality of being wise

Webster—having knowledge and the capacity to make proper use of it

My definition—the ability to see things from God's perspective. Look up James 3:17 and Proverbs 9:10 and 11:2

Ezekiel 28:12 says Satan was full of wisdom…but he chose to go against God's design, which resulted in his wisdom being corrupted. Look at David in 2 Samuel 11. He knew better than to sleep with Bathsheba, but he made some bad decisions that corrupted his wisdom. Sometimes, we may see fellow brothers and sisters struggling in sin and think, "How could they do that?" Satan deceives some of the best of us. This is where *true* friends come in handy. We need them in our lives to speak truth in love even if, and especially when, we don't want to hear it.

Did you know that "you reap what you sow" works both ways? If you're actively seeking God, you'll reap His wisdom, knowledge, and grace. If you're seeking stuff from the world, you'll reap what the world has to offer.

Day 2

Read 1 John 2:12–14 and John 14:6. Do you see a correlation?

Little children—the way—out of hell into heaven, in it for what they get out of it.

Young men—the truth—learning to overcome the enemy, telling themselves no if necessary.

Fathers—the life—have learned to continually live by the life of another, in it for what God gets out of it.

Day 3

What's your slippery slope?

A few years ago, I got T-boned on my way to work. I remember thinking to myself, "That car is going awful fast to be stopping at the red light," and before I could complete that sentence in my head, *bam*. From that time on, even still to this day, I hesitate to go through intersections because I don't want to go through that again.

Once you identify your "slippery slope," you'll be extra careful to notice the warning signs and hopefully prevent it (whatever it is) from happening again.

I used to be into fashion, modeling, and most of all, *shoes*. I'd pick the shoes and build the outfit around them. As I spend time at God's feet, allowing Him to teach me and change my heart, He began to show me that I don't need material possessions to be happy or fulfilled. However, I still fall into that trap sometimes. I went to a baby shower with a bunch of people from that time in my life. They were all dressed so sharp and trendy, so I was really interested in what and who they were wearing. By the time I left, I had convinced myself that when I got home I was going to completely clean out my closet and start over.

Day 4

Lust of the eyes can lead us to act without consulting God first. Read Joshua 7:2–5. Israel goes into battle without first going to God in prayer. They were defeated at Ai and lost thirty-six men. If you keep reading in that chapter, Joshua falls on his face and cries out in prayer. God says, "Get up! You've got sin in the camp."

Can you think of a selfish decision you've made, or maybe a decision made without prayer first, that came with some consequences?

When I left one of my former jobs, I told my boss I was quitting and that my last day was in one week. The start date for the next job was already set, and if I gave him two weeks, I wouldn't have any time off before starting at the next place. After I realized that if I only offered one week I wouldn't get the three weeks' vacation I had, I tried to say I didn't realize it and change my last day. They wouldn't let me, and I lost that 120 days pay. My selfishness led me to be dishonest. That lost pay was the result of me making a bad decision.

If you took inventory of your time throughout one week, how would it look?

When we say we're too busy for something, it's just an excuse for us not *wanting* to do it. We *make* time for what's important to us.

Day 5

What will people remember about you? Will your legacy point people to Him? Or to things that perish (fame, looks, clothing, big house, successful career, etc.)?

Week 2

Did anything stand out to you that you'd like to discuss? Was there anything you hadn't heard before?

Leader questions:
Day 1

Have you interacted with somebody struggling with pride? What did it look like?

I used to work for a guy who lived in plausible deniability. He was determined not to make a decision one way or another so he could always be right.

Day 2

Do you realize that one seemingly simple act of obedience can change many lives?

My friend, Heather, was obedient in asking me to join her for Bible study at her house. From there, we had a great friendship and discussed many Bible studies. During our time together, she invited me to a Lifeway Women's Leadership Forum. It was that conference that inspired this Bible study.

Which would you rather do: obey man-made law so you aren't thrown in the fire, or live by God's word and accept the consequences?

Did you notice that God didn't zap Nebbie right away? He waited a year. Why?

Genesis 6:3—God gave the people of Noah's day 120 years to repent.

From 2 Peter 3:9—"*The Lord is not slow about His promise, as some count slowness, but is patient toward you, not wishing for any to perish but for all to come to repentance.*"

Sometimes, He lets us simmer in our sin because He's being patient.

Can you say, "Thank You, Lord," regardless of your circumstances? In other words, when you're on the side of the road with a flat tire, can you pray in that moment and say, "Thank You, Lord, for this flat tire"? Why or why not? Have you ever thought about it?

I've learned to say, "Thank You, Lord, for my back hurting so bad today because it'll help me appreciate the days when it hurts less."

Day 3

The enemy fills our heads with lies for so long that it's hard to believe the truth about ourselves. Look up John 16:8. Notice the Holy Spirit convicts us of not only sin and judgment but also righteousness. When you're bashing yourself, them's fightin' words! Jesus lives in you, so when you talk bad about your regenerated, forgiven self, you're talking about His family.

If you're spiraling out of control in your head about something, how do you stop it? What's your strategy?

We learn with difficulty but forget with ease.

Day 4

Does position or pay motivate you? What if you don't get either?

What motivates how you work? What makes you go "all in"?

It matters because the enemy loves to get us busy so we "don't have time" to do things, like we talked about last week. If you recognize that you're spending too much time/effort/money on something for the benefit of the world, *get rid of it*.

Day 5

What do you trust in? Recognition from your peers? Your kids' success or popularity? Your financial status? That you're well-known at church?

What's cognitive dissonance?

The principle of being confronted with a state of conflict and deciding if you'll change your action or belief. Example: Smoking is bad. Either you'll believe smoking *is* bad and stop smoking (changing your action), or you'll think it isn't *that* bad and keep smoking (changing your belief).

Can you see how that relates here? Do you really love God, or do you just talk about loving God?

When conflict comes, will you practice what you preach? Or will you compromise?

Week 3

Is anything changing in the way you see sin or temptation?

Day 1

Do you feel necessary in the body of Christ?

If not, do you think it's because the body doesn't need you? Or do you think it's because you're not engaged?

Can you look back over time (last six months, year, three years) and see your spiritual growth?

What does it look like to see things through eternal eyes?

Try and share some real-life examples. This could be as simple as seeing somebody who everybody else looks down on as God's creation and loving them. It could also be understanding that the healing you've been praying for may not come this side of heaven.

Day 2

How's your prayer life? There are no right or wrong answers, but talk it out. You may be surprised at how many different ways we can pray.

What does a *good* prayer life look like?

- Pray before meals
- Pray with family before bed

What does a *great* one look like?

- Pray before meals
- Pray with family before bed
- Pray with prayer team at church
- Asking God to teach you straight from His heart to yours as you spend time in the Word
- When somebody asks you to pray for them, stop right then and do it
- When you feel yourself about to say something you shouldn't, you go to a private place and talk it out with God

Day 3

How are you impacting those around you?

This topic seems out of place. Last week, we talked about how one act of obedience can affect many. This week, we're discussing the other side of the coin: affecting many from an act of disobedience. So, how are you impacting those around you? For Him? Or for the world?

Tell me about your thoughts on this statement: *God's opinion of me is the only one that matters.*

Does that sound right to you? Why or why not?

Day 4

Answers to the matching verses: 1-E, 2-B, 3-A, 4-C, 5-D

Is looking in the past good or bad? Or both?

The Bible talks frequently about insight, in Ephesians and other places. I believe insight is given to us through pain or a difficult situation. It hurts *so* bad that we never want to do it again—like when a kid puts their hand on the hot burner of the stove, even though their parents told them not to. They'll get burned, and it'll hurt for a long time, but they'll never make that mistake again. The only other time I look in the past is to remember what God has brought me through. When He pulls me out of my mess and I'm on the other side of it, I set up a mental altar I can go back to when I'm struggling with something else. It helps me remember that since He got me out of that situation, He can get me out of this one too.

Day 5

Is it hard to share the gospel? If so, why?

- Afraid people will ask questions we don't know the answers to.
- What if someone says they don't believe in Jesus?
- What if they never talk to us again?

How can we combat those fears?

- *Tell 'em you don't know but you'll find out.*
- *Tell 'em you love 'em anyway, and if they change their mind, you'll be glad to talk it out.*
- *That stinks, but aren't you glad you loved them enough to tell 'em anyway?*

Do you think God is mad at you when you sin?

I heard this story, and it makes sense in this context. There was an old couple taking a Sunday drive. They were in the same bench seat boat of a car they'd had their entire marriage, and he's still driving. She says, "Remember when we used to sit so close and hold hands while we traveled?" He replied, "I haven't moved." We're that old lady when we sin. We're the ones who've moved. God hasn't.

When you're experiencing difficulties, can you see that your focus has slipped off Him? If not, do you have a friend who'll tell you as much even if, and especially when, you don't want to hear it?

Week 4

Are you starting to realize that you *can* fight against the enemy's attacks?

Day 1

We teach what we know and that what doesn't kill you makes you stronger. What are some things you've endured that you can use to minister to somebody experiencing the same thing?

Sharing the gospel will look different for everybody. For example, some write songs, some author books, and others preach. Do you know what your outlet is or will be?

When you pray, do you come with a laundry list to a distant person you're hoping to get consolation from? Or do you have genuine conversations with a real person?

Have you ever led anybody to be saved? If you feel comfortable, please share.

Day 2

How is your faith? Like the chair or like the bridge?

After reading Romans 5:3–5 and James 1:2–4, have you noticed the progressions in your own life?

tribulation brings perseverance	testing brings endurance
perseverance brings proven character	endurance brings the perfect result
proven character brings hope	perfect result is our spiritual maturity
hope won't disappoint	

I worked at a company for six years but hated about 4.5 of that time because of how people treated me. I loved my coworkers and felt the need to stay for some reason. After I finally left and got another job, I realized how much I learned during that tough time. I excelled in the next role because of those past experiences.

Day 3

Are you aware that you have the freedom to fail?

I bring this point up because a guy I used to work with was about to mess up. He said, "Sorry in advance," to which I responded, "I won't love you any less if you do." If we never failed at anything, we'd never learn the right way of doing things. God gives us the freedom to fail because He can then teach and change us.

How good are you at recognizing reality over what you feel?

This is a biggie y'all. Spend time here if the conversation is good. When the enemy gets us in our feels, he'll get the victory.

What does it mean to run something through sixty-six books?

It means to take that word or phrase through other verses in the Bible and let the Bible explain itself. If you see something that seems contradictory, there's a good chance it's the translation, your preconceived notions, or what you've been told about that verse. Keep digging until it lines up with the rest of God's word.

Do you ask for forgiveness when you sin, or do you confess your sin and ask Him to teach you how not to do it again?

From 1 Peter 3:18: *"Christ also died for sins once for all."*

Hebrews 10:10—*"We have been sanctified through the offering of the body of Jesus Christ once for all."*

Hebrews 9:23–28 (read it out loud). He's not going back to the cross.

I want to say my next point with compassion because it can sound harsh, but when God revealed this truth to me, it was a game changer. When you mess up at work, does your boss make you reapply for the job? Of course not, right? So, when you sin, why do you ask for something you've already received (forgiveness)?

Don't hear me wrong; confession is vital. When we confess, we start to scoot back over toward the driver's seat and lock hands again (like the old couple in the car).

God already knows what we did and what we're thinking. We don't confess *to be* forgiven. We confess because we *are* forgiven. Confession frees us from guilt, shame, and regret. Once we get it off our chest, we can feel more comfortable around Him again.

Day 4

If I took about thirty minutes to show you some defensive karate moves, then said, "Okay, we're going into a fight; do what I showed you." Could you? Would you feel comfortable?

The Bible is our only weapon. Do you know how to use it? Are you confident using it?

Does it sound easy to resist the enemy so he will flee from you? You do realize that it took Jesus resisting Satan three times for him to flee. And Jesus is the very source of truth!

Do you think it will be easier for us to resist and make the devil flee? Think again, sis. Even if we do manage to stand firm and resist, he'll shoot three flaming arrows at you next time instead of just one. Point of the story, this fight won't be easy. That's why God gave us a Savior who can relate and a helper (the Holy Spirit) who can show us the way.

Day 5

When somebody comes at you sideways, can you see through the defensive response you'd like to give them and recognize why they're so upset?

I'm sure you've heard this expression before, but hurt people hurt people. Having godly discernment is being able to see past the exterior anger to see the interior cause.

Do you think you're attractive? Well, guess what? You are!

Some women are attractive to *some*. Some women are attractive to *most*. Some women are attractive to *all*. We need to do our best not to become the "strange woman" in Proverbs 2.

Have you recognized God changing your desires? Did you used to love something you no longer like to do?

I'd like to end with a prayer.

God, I love You! Thank You for this journey of taking what You've written on my heart and sharing it in a Bible study. I pray over the people who'll read it, that You'll change their lives forever, and that they'll come to it with an open heart that's ready to listen. God, would You allow the brokenness of the world to encourage them to embrace their own faults. May You light a fire in these readers, that they'll want to know You more intimately, daily. Teach them to ask You questions, to beg You for insight, and to not leave until You reveal Yourself to them. God, I pray for that determination in them. Holy Spirit, would You take this printed word and transform it into truth, teach them more about Yourself, and how to hear Your voice on a regular basis. I pray for these ladies to make time for You and let You make real change in their lives. I love You, Lord. Thank You for loving me first. In Jesus's name, amen!

ABOUT THE AUTHOR

After learning the beauty of safety in gymnastics, as a gymnast and coach, Leslee Kiser led the charge for safety as Safety Director for a construction company.

Now, she's focused on protecting hearts.

When God showed her how much He loved her and had done for her, Leslee just couldn't keep it to herself.

www.ingramcontent.com/pod-product-compliance
Lightning Source LLC
Chambersburg PA
CBHW081337120626

46546CB00011B/3379